GOTCHA

COLD CASE

True Crime Stories from the
Detectives Who Solved It

by
BRAD SCHLERF

Brad Schlerf
Houston, TX
BradSchlerf.com

Published by
Elite Online Publishing
63 East 11400 South #230
Sandy, UT 84070
EliteOnlinePublishing.com

ISBN: 978-1-956642-35-3 (Paperback)
ISBN: 978-1-956642-37-7 (eBook)

TRU002010
TRU002000

QUANTITY PURCHASES: Schools, companies, professional groups, clubs, and other organizations may qualify for special terms when ordering quantities of this title. For information, email info@eliteonlinepublishing.com.

TABLE OF CONTENTS

For more information and series
updates visit BradSchlerf.com

DEDICATION

To all my brothers in Blue and Camo, don't let the horrors of the world that we must see and dredge through, define your nature. We must do this so that our loved ones and the rest of America will not have to see them in their front yard.

It has taken me 30 years to write some of these stories and for my family, it will be the first time some of them hear the stories that I would not talk about.

I have been all over the world, and I truly believe we live in the greatest country in the world. I am proud to have defended it, both in the United States Military and as a Law Enforcement Officer, and will continue to do so until my last breath.

Stay strong my brothers.

FOREWORD

We hope this book will help you to gain an understanding and perspective of what our military and law enforcement officers go through on any given day. A perceptive and witty man from Florida whose whole life has been dedicated to community and service. His desire to help make the world a better place led him to join the United States Military which exposed him to death and destruction in the wake of war and what true hate looks like. He continued his life of service in law enforcement only to see inherent evil in what people will do to each other out of greed and the pursuit of power.

PREFACE

Gotcha – Cold Case

This is the first in a 3-book series which walks the reader through the real-life crimes and events of Detective Brad Schlerf. As Brad's career unfolds, so does the Cold Cases featured in this book which encompasses the crimes of one criminal family over 20 years. Detective Schlerf portrays himself in the book using his real undercover name from his days in narcotics. All crimes in this book are real, the names of the characters have been changed to protect the private lives of the officers, and to not give any real credit to the criminals involved.

"Cold Case" walks the reader through the trauma of the death and the anguish of the case going cold. Leads for the case can be found in the most unexpected places, and sometimes come from nowhere.

Rest assured, we will solve these crimes, and we are taking you, the reader, with us as the case unfolds.

CHAPTER 1

LIFE

In January 1992, the cold wind of winter in the small Amish town of Yoder, Kansas, would be a nice reprieve from the heat emanating in the crowded room. Police officers dressed out for the graduation ceremony at the Kansas Law Enforcement Center were waiting excitedly, the air in the room buzzing with anticipation and conversation. Among them, Brad White sat quietly, uniform perfect for graduation with blond hair and perceptive blue eyes taking in the energetic scene around him. Although his face remained stoic, he too was brimming with the excitement that comes from beginning a new journey and hope for the future.

He glanced at his watch and realized the ceremony was about to begin. He glanced over to his shoulder to warn his old roommates sitting behind him, James Christian and Dennis Wolf. All three carpooled to the academy from Junction City, and Grandview Plaza, Kansas together over the past few months to attend their classes. They meshed well together with their military backgrounds in what soon would become lifelong friendships. James an Army Ranger, Dennis an Army Military Police Officer, and Brad in Army Aviation.

The buzz of conversation between cadets and guests halted as the Commissioner of the Academy began to walk to the podium to begin the ceremony. Every eye in the room watched the Commissioner as his hoarse voice filled the small room with words of gratitude to the newest cadets for their service to the various cities from all over Kansas.

As Brad thought about the new service he was about to fulfill, he recalled when he passed the Advanced Aircraft Training, Air Assault, and Airborne schools.

He added three sets of wings to his uniform in his zest for excitement and thrills before his first duty assignment. Now he had traded in his camo uniform for this blue one. After Desert Storm and coming to his last duty station, Fort Riley, he was ready to settle down and live out in the country with his wife of 3 years, Petra. His job working on aircraft for the military wanted him to move from that beautiful peace in Kansas countryside and he had to decide a new fate. He knew that he wanted to continue to serve his country by serving the community and so here he was, a man in blue and ready to help in a new way.

As the Commissioner ended his speech, Brad, and the few other cadets in the first row, rose to receive honors for being at the top of the training class. Standing at a fit 5'10", Brad's crystal blue eyes stared ahead with no hint of nerves. He climbed the stairs to the stage and greeted the Mayor from Junction City.

"Congratulations, Officer White," the mayor said as Brad shook his hand, and with a quick "Thank you, sir" Brad was back to standing in front of his assigned seat.

He was used to being in uncomfortable situations, but the room was relatively warmer after going up on stage and he was ready for some fresh air soon.

As the last honored cadet reached his seat, the rest of the graduating class from Junction City stood. The mayor's voice rang out once more over the room, *"Please lift your right hand for the oath and repeat the words."*

Every officer in the room stood a little taller right then, and Brad's excitement grew a little more for this new career and future as he repeated, *"I do solemnly swear and affirm to support the Constitution and laws of the United States, the Constitution, and laws of the State of Kansas, and faithfully discharge my duties as an officer of the Junction City Municipality."* The mayor closed

the graduation ceremony with a deep, hoarse, *"Congratulations, new officers of the Junction City Police Department,"* and the friends and family in the audience stood and applauded as the new officers threw their caps in the air in celebration.

✪ ✪ ✪

5 MONTHS LATER

Brad spent the months following his graduation gathering information and learning the ropes of Junction City with his training officer, Jeff Giles. It did not take long for Jeff to see that Brad was able to keep his head down and blend in easily with the members of the community, remembering the names and faces of those he would encounter and interact with. Brad took to learning the area easily and made notes often, and Jeff knew that Brad had the fortitude to be an amazing police officer but was a novice to the ways of the street.

On shift late one May evening, the two sat in their patrol car with the glaring streetlights glowing in the black inky night. Jeff was quietly sipping his coffee, watching the late-night traffic on Washington Street as Brad slowly reached for his notepad to start going over things from the last few days. Before Brad could become too engrossed in his work, Jeff asked, *"What made you become a cop, White?"*

Brad closed his notebook and set his pen down as he huffed a laugh. *"Honestly, I just enjoy being the good guy."* Jeff let out a deep laugh.

Brad continued, *"Well, being in the war before this, I've seen things that have prepared me for this career. Growing up in an area that still had degrees of segregation showed me a lot of hate in the world. I grew up learning the values of humanity and I want to see the world be a better place. I want to help make it a better place."* Jeff nodded in understanding. He also had seen some of the worst of humanity, but he too knew it could be better.

"What abo--"? As Brad returned the question, dispatch interrupted the quiet conversation with a loud alert tone over the radio, grabbing the officers' attention in a second.

"Code Blue" a female voice rang over the radio, and as Jeff reached for the radio to respond, the female voice sounded again, *"Code Blue, infant."*

Jeff did a quick nod to Brad, who started fastening his seatbelt, as he responded, *"240 PD en route.*" Jeff hit the lights and sirens, and the patrol car took off towards the address given by dispatch. Soon, they were on Grant Avenue, a stretch of road between Junction City and the military base Fort Riley and could see another patrol car and an ambulance in the distance. Jeff muttered a curse under his breath, shaking his head and said, "*Your first code blue, and it's an infant. The ambulance crew normally handles these medical calls, but we all respond when there is a code blue.*"

Brad looked through the windshield as the trees passed by, his mind bringing up bits and pieces of a soldier's memories. This would not be the first nightmarish thing he would see, and in this line of work, it surely wouldn't be the last. Innocent civilians and children had lain dead at his feet, the cost of war, some would say, but he could remember the feeling of powerlessness, and now he would be able to do whatever he could to help. Brad undid his seatbelt as Jeff pulled up to the trailer and parked near the ambulance.

As Jeff took off over to the ambulance, Brad immediately started scanning the perimeter and looking for anything that seemed out of the ordinary.

Brad took note of the mid-twenties male speaking to another officer near the trailer, and the helpless mother huddled and sobbing on the steps. Brad glanced around the trailer park and noted a few people who were trying to get a glimpse of what all that was about in the rising sunlight. The morning was warming up as Brad moved toward the sobbing mother, he could feel the grass crunch under his boots as he crossed the lawn to the gravel driveway. He approached the sobbing woman, her brown eyes met his blue sympathetic ones, and her sobbing intensified, mascara mixed with tears trailing down her red face framed by frizzy chestnut hair. *"Please make sure my baby is okay!!"*

"My partner is checking on that now, ma'am. While we wait for an update, why don't we go inside so that I can ask you a few questions," Brad said while escorting the woman up the stairs.

Brad opens the front door to the trailer to lead her inside, pushing trash and clothes out of the way with his boots to clear a small path through the living room. The screen door opens, revealing Jeff with the man from the driveway, who promptly walks over to the sobbing brunette and attempts to comfort her sighing, *"Oh, Amanda."*

Jeff turns to Brad, *"This is Gavin Johnson."* Brad starts to write notes on his pad, and Jeff turns to Gavin, *"Sir, are you the father?"* Gavin shakes his head and looks down, and Amanda speaks up through her sobs, *"I met him a couple of months ago in the Hollywood Club."* Brad continues to make notes and assumes she probably works at the local strip club.

"Were you the one who found the baby, ma'am?" Jeff said, but Gavin lifted his head and stated, *"No, I did. I heard the baby crying and woke up. Amanda had a late night, so I was letting her sleep. When I went to check up on the baby, she was choking. I called the paramedics immediately and tried to help the baby and I finally got the penny out when you guys arrived."*

Brad continued to jot his notes taking in the room around him. There was a half-eaten banana with the peel on the counter, an empty bread bag that missed the trash can on the floor, and unwashed laundry next to the fridge.

As Brad was finishing up the notes, Gavin added, *"I tried my best to save her. I just hope she is okay."* Brad glanced up from his notes and studied Gavin's demeanor, and then they heard the stretcher being lifted and carried in by the paramedics.

They stepped out of the way to watch them tend to the small bundle underneath the white sheet while Amanda's sobbing became hysterical as she was crying, *"my baby."* The EMT looked towards Amanda and said, *"We are taking her to the hospital now. There isn't much time. We need to go."*

As they lifted the small baby into the ambulance, Brad could see her small lips turning purple with her chest rapidly rising and falling, attempting to catch a breath that was not coming. He helped Amanda into the ambulance next to her daughter. Suddenly Gavin rushed up to the doors and was stopped by the paramedics. *"Only one person can ride with us there. We can't allow more people than that."*

"He'll ride with us," Brad stated as they started closing the doors, and then the ambulance pulled away, leaving a trail of lights and the sound of sirens fading as they raced towards the hospital. Jeff and Brad led the way to the police cruiser as Gavin followed closely behind, getting in the cruiser's backseat as they began their journey

to the hospital. Both officers were silent for a moment as they took in the black, ominous night that had taken a sad turn that may cost this child her life.

Brad turned to Gavin and asked, *"When did you find the baby?"*

"About half an hour ago. I told Amanda the messy house is a hazard for the baby. She loved that baby so much", Gavin replied.

Brad raised an eyebrow, *"What do you mean about the messy house? I thought it was a penny that stopped her from breathing?"*

Gavin became silent as his face went blank. He turned to Brad and confidently stated, *"Yes, it was a penny.*

Brad slowly nods his head and takes a quick glance at this training officer who is looking at Gavin from the rearview mirror. As the silence once again takes over the ride, Brad stares through the windshield and sees the bright lights from the hospital coming up in front of them. Jeff makes quick work of parking the cruiser, and the three of them walk briskly inside with Gavin leading the way.

As they entered the building, they saw Amanda's small frame. She looked up at the sound of their footsteps approaching. Mascara was running down her delicate face with sad brown eyes, red and puffy from crying. She started crying again as she saw her boyfriend and the officers. Gavin immediately takes her into his arms, head cradled against her chest as she continues to cry and pray that her child will be alright.

Brad and Jeff stand in the distance as the doctor comes through the emergency doors to talk to the worried mother, and although they are too far to hear, they know that the baby did not make it. A shake of the head from the physician immediately created a grief-stricken how from Amanda heard throughout the hallway as her world broke quickly and fell apart.

Walking back to the cruiser, Giles asks Brad, *"So, what did you think?"*

"Unfortunate accident is what it looks like. Gavin seems odd, although the EMS did recover a penny from the baby's throat. There is not anything we can do from here", Brad said.

Jeff nods his head in agreement, gets in the car, and starts it up. Brad joins him as the car roars to life, and soon they are back on the street, orange lights now giving way to the rising sun and the end of their shift.

✪   ✪   ✪

That morning, as the sun began to stream through the window of his country home, Brad thought over the difficulties of the night. The child's death was ruled an accident, but he felt deep down that there was more to the story. He looked out the window and sighed, knowing that he still had a lot to learn about being a police officer. What he doesn't know is how important this one incident would be to a future case. He would revisit this case later, much later, if only someone had known.

CHAPTER 2

THE NEXT CASE

B y the end of the year, Brad was well on his way to advancing his career although the thrill of working for the concept of justice had just begun. The case of the baby with the dislodged penny was closed, ruled as an accident, and Brad moved on to other cases.

Jeff recognized his partner's ability to handle complicated cases, so Brad was placed in surveillance detail for the drug task force. Being new to the department and living in the country, he was virtually unknown in town. He had the ability to blend in on the street, which gave him the leverage needed to get into the undercover work. He began in small roles, working out of a rundown apartment building in the hood, taking photos of the players in the park, and documenting the activity. With his keen observations, it eventually landed him more frequent positions in the Drug Task Force cases. Soon, he was actively assisting in narcotic cases. Brad worked long hard hours learning and understanding the intelligence aspects of tracing calls, identifying callers, tracking them on PenLink, and mapping out how they fit into the criminal puzzle.

In Brad's quest to work for justice and the search for the truth, he also discovered a fondness for the adrenaline of apprehending suspects. His time on the force had earned him a nickname on the streets. The gangs, dealers, and frequent criminals would give officers a street name who were known to disrupt the flow of business. On one particular shift, Brad was chasing a known gang member on foot, and while he was attempting to detain the resisting gang member on the hood of the unmarked car, things didn't go as planned.

Unbeknownst to Brad, his car had been detailed by local inmates trying to earn brownie points as trustees. So, as Brad went to detain the gang member on the hood, the young man slid all the way across and fell to the ground on the other side of the car. Other gang members in the area witnessing the event from then on out referred to him as "Chuck Norris," and the name stuck with Brad for quite sometime after that. The days moved fast, and his passion for this new line of work continued to grow as he learned new aspects to his career and continued to build his skills and a reputation as a good cop.

✪   ✪   ✪

One snowy night while on patrol duties around Christmas, Brad was enjoying a rare moment. He was given a few extra minutes for his dinner break to have a meal with his wife. As part of the life of a cop, a single phone call can change the mood from a joyous, peaceful dinner to one of urgency. The disrupting alert tone immediately shifted Brad's demeanor from relaxed to that of an officer back on-duty. His wife knew that the evening they were sharing was over, which was soon confirmed.

Brad said, *"230 PD en route."* As he walked out the door to get to the car, he kissed his wife goodbye and tried not to look at the disappointment etched in his wife's face as he got into the patrol car.

"Any further details?", he asked dispatch as he pulled out of the drive.

"A Woman called in from out of state, her daughter is married to a soldier, and they were fighting while she was talking to her on the phone. The line went dead, and now they are unable to reach her."

"This can't be good," Brad said to himself in the car, shaking his head and pulling onto the street. Ironic, just minutes ago, he had been trying to enjoy the peace of his family, and now he was driving toward a domestic dispute. The Christmas lights twinkled through the darkness, and Brad recalled the peace with his family was a twinkle in the darkness as he continued to pull his thoughts together as he drove to the address provided by dispatch.

He pulled up to the house which was relatively quiet. Checking the area for anything out of the ordinary, he walked up to the house, noticing Christmas decorations lining the quiet, residential street. Nothing appeared out of the ordinary. Brad approached the small house; an old military housing bungalow left over from World War II moved into the area to create a housing community. The bungalow had two small windows on either side of the door with no sign of life within. He could see the glow of the lights from the Christmas tree twinkling off the glass in the windows but heard nothing but silence from within. He knocked on the door and listened carefully for any signs of activity within the house, but silence was all he heard.

Brad tried his luck again, this time with a solid police officer knocking on the front door. Finally, he was able to hear the thump of footsteps against a wood floor. The footsteps continued past the door into the room left of the door and then back toward the door.

After a minute, the door opened slightly. A man's face protruded through the small opening displaying military cut brown hair and green eyes which immediately met Brad's eyes with a look of concern. Brad glanced past the man as he opened the door, and even though the opening was less than 3 inches wide, he saw a petite brunette standing at the far end of the house, her eyes wide with fear.

"Can I help you?", the soldier asked, attempting to bring Brad's attention back to him in the doorway.

"Ma'am, are you alright?" Brad asked, ignoring the soldier in front of him. Everything went into slow motion as the woman screamed, *"He has a gun behind the door!"*

Brad's mind immediately raced into action. With adrenaline kicking in, he moved his hand to his weapon at his side. The man moved to push the door closed in Brad's face, but Brad was faster. He leaned into the door and placed his foot in the jam to prevent it from closing. Brad adjusted his body and aimed his service weapon at the only part of the man he could see, his face. Their eyes met, and the tension between the two men was palpable as Brad gathered his composure to issue instructions to deescalate the situation.

"Slowly, using two fingers on the barrel, put the gun on the ground, hands away from the trigger."

Brad's intensity was so strong it seemed as if time was standing still. He noticed the hammer of his own weapon slowly easing back from the tension on the trigger. It seemed to slow down further until he saw the barrel of the shotgun being handed to him with two fingers as he instructed. With his left hand, Brad seized the shotgun, holstered his weapon with his right hand and forced the door open with his shoulder.

"Face the wall and hands on top of your head," he ordered as he made his way into the house and secured the shotgun firmly. He could see the small woman more clearly now but could not see any physical signs of injuries. He again asked if she was okay to confirm his observations. *"Yes, we were just arguing,"* she said quietly, her eyes glancing down.

The static of Brad's radio sounded, and dispatch rang out, *"PD to 230 checking."* This was dispatch checking to make sure the situation was under control since Brad had not advised if he had contacted the occupants. Brad replied, *"10-4"*, then relayed the information to dispatch, who responded that the soldier's 1st Sergeant had been contacted and was en route to take the soldier back to post.

Brad cleared the weapon he took from the soldier, broke open the single-shot breech, and a yellow cartridge ejected from the shotgun hitting the floor, rolling toward the lit tree. Brad shook his head, looked at the soldier and told him, *"The military can deal with you now"*, securing his hands behind his back.

Brad did not arrest him since there were no injuries, no signs of physical violence, and the soldier never pointed the gun at him or threatened to use it. All he could do was wait patiently at the house until the chain of command came to collect the soldier, as his eyes fell upon a shadow in the lights of the Christmas tree.

Brad's heart dropped to the floor as he saw slowly from behind the tree a little girl no more than three emerged from the light. She reached down and picked up the ejected cartridge on the floor, looking at her mother with scared eyes and trembling lips. She then approached her mother with a large hug. Once again, Brad asked if they were both okay as the woman wept and gathered up her little girl.

"Yes, thank you," she said as she sobbed, rocking her daughter back and forth, clutching her tightly.

Brad turned his attention back to the soldier and said, *"I could have shot you right in front of your little girl."*

That night, once the soldier's chain of command had taken him back to post, some of the bitter reality of his job truly hit him, and he realized that this would probably not be the only time something like this would happen.

✪   ✪   ✪

As his career progressed, his personal life began to show the strain of the reality of a police officer's life. Each decision he made did not just affect him, but his wife's life as well. Even though he was reluctant to share the details of the horrors he witnessed, she still was not happy with the chances he took.

"It's too dangerous," Petra would say, just to be met with his determination and adrenaline-filled satisfaction that he was doing the right thing. Although he did enjoy the thrill of the chase and apprehending subjects, he kept reminding himself he was in it to make the world a better place. The scene with the soldier and his wife was something that he never forgot. The fear in the daughter's eyes stuck with him, and he knew he wanted to continue to help people. This job was not asking anything of him that he had not experienced before. High-risk situations and risking his life were something he was doing day in and day out while serving in the military, yet this was somehow different.

After these conversations with his wife, he would often sit up thinking about his time in the Army, and although it seemed like so long ago, it had only been a couple of years. His mind still drifted back to nights in muddy pathways, with rows of tents and the smell of filth and despair. Sometimes the echoing sounds of missiles drifted through his ears transporting him back to the desert instead of home with his wife.

There were times where death had gotten too close. Brad remembered one occurrence in Dhahran during a daily missile alert. He clearly remembered putting on his chemical gear as the alarms sounded while he was in the staging camp. Moments later, the warehouse he was in shook with the reverberations of an explosion. This one was close, and although it was the middle of the day, the sky was dark with dust, and a strange new smell in the air as debris fell on the tin roof of the warehouse.

Soldiers ran out of the warehouse where they were assembling the aircraft, making them ready to fly to their battle camps. They found that a patriot missile had shot down yet another scud missile, and now pieces of missiles rained down on them as the exploded missile was directly overhead when it was destroyed. On this occasion, he had to drag a young soldier back inside after he freaked out and started firing his M16 into the sky at the missiles overhead.

The chaos of the day remained in his head, and although no one had ever talked about the incident, they pushed through. He continued to reassure his wife that he would be fine when he woke from nightmares. She had seen him through his deployments in the military, but she truly did not know the extent of everything that had happened in the desert.

Had Petra known much worse things had happened there, and there were more to come as an officer, she would have fled right then.

Brad continued to excel in his patrol duties and often found himself being tasked with undercover roles. As the D.A.R.E program was born he would turn towards interactions with kids in the community and talk to them about drug prevention. Utilizing his ability to empathize with the potential gang members, he would gain insight into dealers in the area, finding ways to relate to their situations, and determine the motivation of what led them into their lifestyle. He discovered many gang members needed the sense of "belonging as a family" to an organization that kept them bonded with the group.

During his work with the kids and D.A.R.E. officers, one day he was called up to the Chief's office. Brad walked toward the office, truly perplexed. Being called to the boss's office was never a good thing, but as he greeted the Chief, his trepidation was replaced with curiosity as the Chief smiled at him.

"I'm sure you're wondering why I called you in today. I hear good news about your time here

with us so far. Your memory skills have proven quite useful within the department, and I hear nothing but great things about how hard you work. The Sergeant from narcotics explained that you have been memorizing the local juvenile offenders, hangouts, vehicles, and who they are associating with. He said they seem to start singing when you are asked to identify them as they so often provide false names."

The Chief gestured for Brad to take a seat and then followed suit. *"Thank you, sir,"* Brad replied. *"Yeah, they don't know what to think when I tell them I am going to tell their grandmother what they are up to or maybe their girlfriend's parents."*

The Chief raised his hand, cutting Brad off. Brad in turn watched him carefully, eager to know where this was heading, although he did not have to wait long.

"We've changed your duty assignment, White."

Brad's face remained the same, and he waited silently for the Chief to give him the details, and he watched as an embossed inter-office document on Official Police letterhead landed on the table and was slid toward him.

The chief continued. *"After careful evaluation, we believe that you are best suited as the department Gang Intelligence Officer, and we have made it official. This new position will require you to track and identify the gangs in the area, along with an understanding of their movements. As your work has been exemplary in your current assignment, we are expecting the same dedication into this new assignment."*

A thud sounded as a thick folder landed on the desk. *"This folder has the first group."*

Brad opened the document and scanned through the monochrome photographs, flipping through pictures of kids, some younger than thirteen years old. Brad stopped and went back to the first page on top and continued to stare at the picture of the young teen boy. The boy was no more than 15, but his deep brown eyes stared back at him with far more age than his face showed.

The Chief continued, *"It is dangerous, but we are aiming to decrease the number of gang members, especially in schools. Are you up for the new assignment?"*

Brad's eyes continued to linger on the photograph, and the Chief added, *"He was arrested for murder and is currently in the juvenile detention center."*

"I'll do it," Brad responded as he stood to shake the Chief's hand. As he closed the door behind him, he heard the Chief say, *"Good luck."*

✪ ✪ ✪

The next few years, his career took several turns. He had to testify against several gang members, some far too young. He was also able to celebrate the success of solving multiple cases, with a cost to professional success. Now, he sat in his apartment alone and stared at the picture of his two-year-old daughter, Anne, beautiful with his wife's brown hair and his piercing blue eyes. He sighed sadly, thinking about the distance between them now. As is the case with most police officers' spouses, she couldn't handle the hours and the constant worry, and it had been a year since the divorce, but he still felt a hole in his life.

Rather than sulking, he continued his determined career path without his wife for the thrill of fighting crime and finding justice. Although this was not the success trail, he hoped it would be originally, he knew he was on the correct twisty road he was destined for with his skill set. His impeccable teamwork with officers, teachers, and prosecutors during his time as a Gang Intelligence Officer had led to a significant decrease of openly active gang members within the school system, just as they had intended, and Brad finally felt as though he was ready for the next step. With the recent changes in his personal life, he was starting to feel complacent, and he began to seek out other opportunities to ignite his ambition with an adrenaline rush.

On April 19, 1995, Brad was summoned once again into the Chief's office. As soon as he entered the room, he could feel the urgency and tension in the air. He straightened completely as he glanced toward two men who stood in the corner of the room, both wearing a suit and tie exuding an air of authority.

The chief looked up at him from his desk and stood up, *"White, I'd like to introduce you to Agents Miller and Jones with the FBI"*.

As the men shook hands with Brad, the chief continued, *"They have a suspect for the bombing that has just occurred in Oklahoma City, and they need our assistance. I'm assigning you to them as a liaison to help them navigate our city, and coordinate any assistance needed."*

Timothy McVeigh, who was already behind bars for speeding without a license plate and carrying a concealed weapon, ended up being responsible for the deaths of over 168 adults and children in the Oklahoma City bombing.

Brad was brought up to speed with McVeigh's connection to Junction City by the Agents. They knew that they had to start their investigation with McVeigh's movements leading up to the explosion, and who he had been in contact with to determine if they were looking at additional bombs or targets. They had to be sure this would never happen anywhere else.

Brad and the agents from the FBI soon learned that McVeigh had constructed the homemade bomb, created it with a fuse of fertilizer, diesel fuel, and other materials he had acquired from local businesses in Junction City during his time in Fort Riley. The rental truck which housed the bomb was also rented from a local business, and the plan seemed coordinated from a local motel.

As Brad reviewed the footage from the horrific bombing, he recalled his time in the military.

The bombing, destruction, and chaos were saddening, and so many lives were changed irrevocably that day. Brad knew that he had to continue putting his skills to use in making sure that he could do whatever was in his ability to make the world just a bit of a better place.

His work with the FBI in the OKC bombing case had earned him a reputation for details he continued to build on over the next few years with Junction City PD. While working undercover one night at a country club, he found the love of his life. She was dancing in Rocky jeans with brown hair and excited blue eyes. He found himself mesmerized and just could not look away.

"Her name is Marie," the bartender said following his gaze.

"I didn't ask," responded Brad.

Laughing, the bartender said, *"When you stare like that, you look like a creep."*

Brad laughed and patiently sipped on his drink. Soon enough, he had the chance to approach her, and before long he had spent the whole night talking and laughing with her, like he had never done before.

"Marie is a beautiful name," Brad said as she leaned into him laughing.

She smiled and coyly whispered, *"It's not my real name."*

Brad's investigative senses kicked in. Did the bartender give him the wrong name? She was not a stripper providing a fake name, was she? No, she held herself way too proudly and seemed like she was just at the club to dance and enjoy the music.

Marie's joyful and mischievous eyes met his alert and candid stare, *"You wouldn't be able to figure out my real name because all my life, I've gone by my nickname given to me by my parents. But I will make a deal with you. If you can guess my name, I will go out on a date with you."*

With a wink, she finished her drink, and Brad could only stare as she walked away.

Brad knew that Marie was special, and he knew that she was interested in him- which was a major plus.

Although Marie was sure Brad would never figure out her name, she also did not know that he was an intelligence officer.

It was not long before Brad got the date with Marie he had bargained for by discovering her real name. After all, he was keen on finding out any information he needed to crack cases. Their relationship continued smoothly from that point on, but of course, Brad knew from experience the effects of his chosen career with relationships.

His work with JCPD provided Brad with the growth and experience he needed to advance as an officer, while also helping Marie understand what a romantically involved relationship with a police officer really was like.

Early in their relationship, Brad asked Marie to drop him off in one of the nice residential neighborhoods in town so he could walk to work. He was working out of a house that seemed boarded up for construction, but he had been using it as a decoy office while he was looking into some possibly corrupt officers, attorneys, and maybe even a judge. There were only three people who knew what Brad was doing.

His fellow officers were informed that he was on disciplinary leave. They were told he had recently made an arrest where the subject had gotten a little beat up and "Chuck Norris" was under disciplinary investigation. It wasn't even close to the truth, but with his noticeable absence from the police department it was believable.

The investigation had taken a turn, two attorneys were discovered to have a cocaine habit, missing money from drug seizures, a cop that might have tipped off a dealer before a raid, and a judge who was in the middle of it all. It was a huge case, and Brad was not sure what he had gotten himself into. He was tracing the calls between the dealers, the attorneys, and the officer, but one thing was for sure. It was not going to end well for quite a few people.

A few weeks later, Brad handed Marie an envelope with the name and address of a KBI Agent on the front in print, and his instructions scared the life out of her.

He looked into her beautiful blue eyes as he placed the brown envelope in her small hand. *"Take this envelope and put it somewhere safe. If I don't come home or call you after this weekend, take it to the address on the cover."* He kissed her goodbye and went to work.

He came home after a long weekend, and Marie had no idea where he had been. She waited a bit and asked about the envelope and if everything was okay. Brad just reassured her that everything was fine, and they went about their day.

A few short nights later, he got called into the District Attorney's office. Brad thought it was strange since they generally do not work at night. The hair stood on the back of his neck as he walked through the parking lot on the moonless night listening to the crickets outside. As he approached the entryway of the building, he noticed the Chief of Police standing on the other side of the glass doors.

The Chief stood tall still in his dark suit despite the late hour and said, *"We have an issue, White, the Drug Task force attorney you identified has been shot."*

Brad's face immediately shifted to concern, and the Chief continued. *"He will survive, but something doesn't seem right."*

Brad listened intently as the Chief relayed more information. The attorney had been shot on a country road near Riley, Kansas just a few hours earlier. The car was found with multiple gunshots in the hood and windshield, and the driver was taken by ambulance to the hospital. KBI Agents were interviewing him in a private hospital room as they were speaking.

They soon learned the injured attorney was, in fact, skimming money from the drug seizures. His cocaine habit had him making deals with the dealers that were supposed to be arrested. A pair of the dealers had staged the shooting of the attorney's car and it had been reported as an attempted HIT. In an effort to make it look real, it may have been an accident or maybe it truly was an attempt to silence the attorney, but the shots were directed all over the windshield except one shot. That one shot was a straight shot into the driver's area, and the attorney was hit. A bullet hole in his jacket and another in the badge wallet he kept in his pocket showed the path. The round, a 22, was found lodged into the badge and amazingly stopped the bullet from fatally striking him in the chest.

Normally an attorney does not get issued a badge, but the task force attorney was so often on crime scenes he insisted on having a badge to make himself more official. Whether this was coincidence or part of a long play scheme no one will ever know but either way it scared him and it was not long before he started talking. He released the names of each person involved and their role with all the pieces fitting together.

Brad was pleased to learn that the officer and the judge seemed to be clueless as to the complexity of the thefts and drug usage, and in the end, they were cleared of all involvement in the crime. The attorneys were subsequently disbarred and currently, they are working as private counsel with no standing as attorneys in the State of Kansas.

✪　✪　✪

As Brad's personal life began to flourish, he found himself working with a new partner who was better known as "Smokey," because he always had a cigarette in his hand.

With a warm smile and kind brown eyes, Smokey was a seasoned officer from a military police background who kept intel on everything. He had a knack for talking to the youth and others with an approachable energy that allowed people to open up to him. It took Brad a bit of observation time to learn his secret. Smokey refused to speak down to people. Unlike a lot of cops, Smokey approached people on equal ground. He treated everyone equally and although he was gentle, understanding, and empathetic, he had a deep gravelly voice that was still firm, almost commanding of respect. Brad learned this listening skill to improve his communication with the people in the community as well, remembering Smokey's voice telling him, "Just shut up and listen".

Although Brad hated riding in Smokey's car because of his smoking, he knew Smokey was one of the most exceptional officers to respond to calls with. When you were on a call with Smokey you knew that the situation would be de-escalated appropriately unless something changed, and it was necessary to use other tactics of response.

In the early summer of 1995, Brad got up and started his usual routine before his shift. As he prepared for work, he could not help but feel this sense of foreboding surrounding him. The air felt thick and heavy with an increased feeling of dread hanging low. Brad was concerned and hopeful that whatever it was, he would be prepared for it. But when he arrived at work the feeling seemed to intensify with a solemnness in the air, no cheerful greeting, the chief wasn't in his office, and most importantly Smokey didn't have his normal box of donuts sitting on the desk for the guys in the precinct.

Brad went to his desk but as he sat down his buddy Dennis walked up with a grave face and said, *"It's Smokey"*.

He knew this was the dread he felt in his stomach before he got to the office. Before he could ask what happened, Dennis said, *"He didn't show up for work this morning, so we sent an officer to his house to check on him. We found him dead this morning, they think it was a stroke."*

Brad's heart sank low in his stomach, and he turned toward Smokey's empty seat, which was normally surrounded by smoke and had the sound of Smokey's gravelly laugh around it. Now it was just a black hole, just the gaping absence of his friend and mentor, and he knew that hole would never be filled the same again.

The funeral procession took place the next day. Officers with the black band on their badge carried his coffin across the bright green grass. With his fiancé, Marie, on his arm, Brad was introduced to the haunting sound of bagpipes at a funeral full of officers reflecting on their morality and the cost of the job.

Brad held his emotions at bay as he watched his mentor's casket being lowered into the ground, buried with military honors. One by one officers who knew Smokey walked up, full of emotion to share their stories of how Smokey had touched all of their lives with their final words to their brother in blue, the procession finished with bagpipes and a 21-gun salute.

Marie remained silent for almost two days after Smokey's funeral. Their wedding would be soon, and this was the first time she saw firsthand the danger in her future husband's job. She began to contemplate what life was like as a police officer's wife would truly encompass. She had two children of her own to think about, and she never thought in a million years she would fall in love with a soldier, or a police officer and she had both in one man. Was she up for the challenge? It takes intense understanding to have a lasting relationship with a cop and being able to handle the baggage that came with that career was a lot.

The day of the wedding approached. Marie and Brad made their vows to keep each other forever and always. As Brad accepted her two children, Lee and Joy, as his own, Marie accepted Anne (from Brad's previous marriage) as her own, and they became a new family.

His personal life finally was becoming what he had envisioned for himself with his amazing family by his side. Life was finally giving him that balance he was looking for in his personal and professional life.

Soon after Brad received an offer from the Riley County Police Department. He was ready to move on to the next stage of his life in a new professional role. He accepted the challenge with vigor.

CHAPTER 3

BUILDING A CAREER

B rad's work at RCPD started just like any other newly hired officer. He had experience under his belt, but he had to pay his dues in the new department before he could move up the ladder. He was ready to take on this role with the same passion and determination as before. He was ready to pay his dues and prove that he was ready for the next step in his career.

The morning of his first shift, he was again called to the Director's office for a meeting. The Director was similar to a Chief but voted in by a Law Board, not the county's people. The Director, a man in his late 60's, with a slightly wrinkled suit, raised a white eyebrow at Brad as he entered the office.

"Good morning, sir, Officer Brad White, reporting as requested." The Director stood and shook his hand.

"Yes, White. It is good to have you on board. Have a seat."

Brad sat alertly in the chair in front of the desk once the Director had seated himself in his chair. The Director began with a brief introduction before he got to what would be required of Brad in this agency.

"So, I will be on patrol?", Brad clarified as soon as the Director finished. Brad was aiming for Detective and the RCPD knew it. He was all for paying his dues, he respected the process, but he did not want to be on patrol for long if he could do anything about it.

"For now, yes. We are pairing you with a seasoned officer, Art Johnston." The Director nodded at someone through the window, and the door opened and a tall, fit man in a crisp uniform soon entered, nodded at Brad, and then stood by the door.

"Brad, I'd like to introduce you to your training officer, Art Johnston," the Director said and once the men shook hands and had acquainted themselves, Brad was briefed on his new role and he and his new partner went to get familiar with the patrol division.

Brad learned that Art was a nice enough guy, but he had a very bitter disposition about the politics involved in law enforcement. Brad, now in a much larger agency, also soon came to realize that most people do not understand how the police are judged on every action and every word they speak.

The lack of cell phones at the time resulted in little to no footage of situations, unlike complaints today. The complaints often were physical complaints of the use of force or officers not being friendly. Police were automatically presumed guilty until proven that they were not responsible for the action or until their perspective justified their actions. Most of these complaints ended with the officer being forced to take a random day off without pay or forced to use earned leave to cover the time off. It was a major responsibility to keep off the blotter report and this brought about a discipline to the force, which ensures that the code of conduct expected of them is maintained. Because of this, Art was burned quite a few times by the administration.

Typically, Brad's initial training would take a few months with a test at the end of each section of training to ensure that the new recruit was qualified to be on their own. The recruits were required to test on state laws, city and municipal laws, county ordinances, as well as the use of the force continuum, geographic landmarks, and maps. Brad always considered himself a man of morals, but he challenged the system and requested to test out of training after only two weeks.

Brad approached Art after his tests, *"Sorry, Art, but that is all I could handle. I need to be out on my own, working cases my way"*, he said as he walked away.

Brad faced challenges navigating around the city of Manhattan, KS, since it was triple the size of

Junction City. RCPD was unique since the cities in the county had gotten together and decided to form a county-wide police department rather than smaller departments. This made the Riley County Police Department the first consolidated and accredited police department in the state of Kansas.

In addition to working patrol in a much larger city, he had the smaller towns and country areas to work as well. Brad was excited and ambitious and ready to take on his new territory.

Brad originally attempted to map the areas out, but with such an overwhelming size difference, he decided to skip the majority of the geographic focus and moved on to something much more to his liking. He soon found that he preferred the people of the small towns compared to the hustle and bustle of Manhattan, and he often volunteered to work patrol assignments in the small surrounding towns of Ogden, Riley, and Leonardville.

The pace that he started for himself at JCPD soon was carried over into Riley County, and he was not just content with working assignments but wanted to interact with the community. This was what he was born to do. He would often get out of his patrol car and walk through the small neighborhoods and play basketball with the kids. Families invited him over for BBQ cookouts and get-togethers. He used the community strategy he learned from Smokey to understand more about who was getting into trouble without getting the police involved.

Soon Brad began working a new shift under a new Sergeant with an old country boy demeanor, SGT Joe Beck. Joe was a lot like Smokey. He was well-liked and respected for his calm way with people. He found a new trust in Joe, and Brad continued to learn more from how he handled situations and spoke to people.

Brad was once again brought into the harsh reality of the dangers of his job in 1998, breaking up a bar fight that resulted in Joe taking a beer bottle to the head. Although he was fine and went about the rest of his shift, Joe was found dead in his country home a few short days later, one boot on his foot, half ready for work. It was later determined that he succumbed to a stroke while getting ready for work. No one really knew if it was from natural causes or the beer bottle to the head a few days earlier.

He had seen death before, and he would see death again, but when it was a brother in blue, the true harshness of the dangers of his job was hard to shake from the forefront of his mind. He tried to push it into the corner, like a little box in the back of his mind that remained closed while on duty. The memories of a lost friend, a mentor, the thoughts of morality remain there sometimes, in that box in the back of his mind, covered in cobwebs from pushing it back for so long.

It has now reopened since Smokey's death with his worries once again flooding his mind. He couldn't help but think about his wife and children at home. They needed him, and he was determined to carry on.

✪ ✪ ✪

Soon after Joe's death, he found himself again on the hunt for the adrenaline that came along with apprehending suspects.

He and a fellow officer, Troy, would do a daily challenge and whoever could make the biggest case or had the most arrests in a single shift won. Brad and Troy would get a list of the outstanding warrants in their assigned areas and then head out to look for them. The warrant division was responsible for finding them during the day and giving intel to the officers so that they could look for them at night. When the shift was slow with regular calls, Troy and Brad would head out and pick up two to four people on outstanding warrants each. Soon, Brad understood that by paying attention to happenings in the street would land him a big case. One particular incident in a rural area got him in the line of sight for the Investigation Division.

(Kansas wild marijuana fields)

Wild marijuana grew in all different areas around the railroad tracks in the country, and drug dealers from all over would come to these areas to pick the wild marijuana buds. They would use the ditch weed to mix with their regular product to increase their yield and profit margins. Too much ditch weed would make people sick rather than high, but this was all about profits.

Brad had been on patrol near the Manhattan mall one day when his eyes caught a black car with a paper tag, blasting music into the quiet peace of the morning. Manhattan had passed an ordinance on loud music, and Brad went on alert as he went to follow the vehicle. Inside was a young male driver with two young female passengers. As he pulled behind the black car, something seemed off about the paper tag and it seemed as though the date had been altered. Brad lit up his red and blues and directed the car to pull over at the entrance of the mall parking lot to avoid traffic issues. Brad slowly stepped out of his patrol car and approached the vehicle, noticing scratched paint on the bumper and a dent by the passenger door as if the driver was not a very cautious driver. He approached the driver's side and motioned for the man to roll his window down.

Before Brad could begin to ask for license and registration, he was greeted by the overwhelming scent of marijuana coming from the car. He immediately stepped back and instinctually placed his hand on his holster, *"Please step out of the vehicle, sir."*

Brad slowly stepped back from the vehicle as the driver emerged, a rolled cigarette dropping to the ground at his feet. Brad said, *"Slowly step out and place your hands on your head."*

He detained the driver, tall and skinny. His white oversized shirt reeked of marijuana, and Brad sat him on the curb to continue with the passengers. As he approached the vehicle again, he noticed that the two teenage girls, no more than sixteen years old. They looked terrified and slightly disoriented, and out of touch with the situation. He removed them from the vehicle and had them sit on the curb so that he could search the vehicle. The vehicle was void of any paraphernalia other than that which fell directly at the driver's feet.

After the girls were identified, they were let go, but Brad escorted the driver to the county jail to conduct the booking process. The driver kept changing information each time Brad asked about his lack of a drivers' license and changed his story and even his name. Soon a detective arrived to take over the case, and Brad was allowed to return to his duties.

As soon as Brad got into his car, he decided the best course of action would be to return to where the arrest was made before the tow truck took the car away. Brad immediately saw the car as he pulled to the entrance, thankful that they had not yet towed the car. He went to do a second sweep of the vehicle when something caught his attention, a Kansas State college ID under the passenger seat. The morning had progressed and with that the area had become busier, but Brad tried to block out the noise of the shoppers and cars around him and pulled the ID out with his tweezers and examined it in the light. Placing the evidence in a bag he asked dispatch to run the card and found that the ID had been reported stolen awhile back and he made the decision to return to the driver at the jail.

Once he reached the precinct, Brad made a beeline for the interrogation area to see if he could find the detective. He turned the corner to see the dark-suited young man from earlier outside of a door filling out some paperwork.

"Excuse me, Detective, I'm Officer White", Brad said as he approached.

Determined, he shook the detective's hand and responded, *"I remember, I'm Detective Rich Fleck".*

"Have you figured out who he is yet", Brad asked and handed the detective the ID card within the evidence bag.

"I found this in his car, under the seat. It came back stolen, reported by the student a while back."

The sharp green eyes of the detective studied the ID and the lines between his dark brows deepened.

"Hmmm...There has been an increase in reports of ID cards lost and stolen in Aggieville, lately." Brad's mind immediately pictured the busy couple of blocks outside of Kansas State University that hosted a variety of bars, restaurants, and shops.

"Do you mind if I speak to the suspect, detective," Brad asked.

The detective shrugged and opened the door, and Brad entered the plain room. His blue patrol uniform seemed almost bright next to the detective's almost dull black suit. The detective did not follow him into the interrogation room.

Brad heard the soft click of the latch as the door closed. Brad looked at the young man from the car who sat hunched in the chair, looking shorter and younger than before. Bloodshot golden-brown eyes flitted over through his shaggy brown hair as he tried to look quietly at Brad. The young man seemed to hunch a little lower in the plain plastic chair, cuffed hands resting in his lap. Brad sat across from the suspect, ignoring the feel of the detective's eyes from behind the glass on him as he began to interrogate the suspect. The young man continued to lie about his name and information and the only thing that Brad even believed to be true was that he had moved to this area from Corpus Christi, Texas.

"Well, if you can't provide me with information that I can verify, I am going to take your fingerprints," Brad stated as he grabbed an ink stamp and print card. Once Brad had finished recording the man's prints, he directed him to stay put and went to meet the waiting detective outside of the door.

They promptly sent the prints to be checked with the Corpus Christi Police Department in Texas and received a faxed photo the CCPD had on file. The picture did not help much since the fax machine had created a blob in place of where the image should have been.

Brad returned to interrogate the suspect further. The suspect would not budge about his name, even with cuffed hands fidgeting and tapping against the scratched table in front of him.

"It is my name, and I can prove it," he said as he reached his cuffed hands behind his head and started pulling up his oversized shirt in the back.

"I have it tattooed on my back."

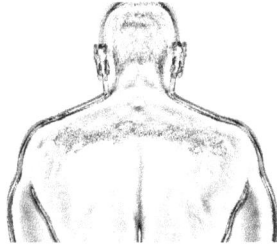

Brad rose and walked behind the man and there was no mistaking the name across his upper back in big block lettering. Brad took out his small notebook and pen and jotted it down to share with Detective Fleck.

Days later, they discovered the suspect Brad had arrested in the vehicle was a gang member in Texas suspected of running drugs back and forth to Nebraska. Detective Fleck invited Brad to work on the leads with him, and soon, they were able to uncover members of the gang working as doormen in the local bars. They would steal the ID cards from the students frequenting the bars and create fake identities.

Brad and Detective Fleck continued to work all the leads involved, turning up nothing but a dead end. After a few days, they discovered that gang members were using the stolen identities to create bank accounts, rent cars, lease apartments, and obtain storage units. Brad continued to put his nose to the grindstone on the case and found one of the storage units was associated with one of the stolen identities.

Anticipation filled the air of the car as Brad rode out to the storage unit with Detective Fleck, knowing this was going to be a big break in the case. Once they gained access to the unit and got the door opened, they discovered copious amounts of methamphetamine and marijuana which was being transported between Texas and northern states.

It wasn't easy to put an end to the entire operation, but Brad continued to work diligently with Detective Fleck to finish the job. They were finally able to build a strong case against all the gang members in several states and shut down the entire pipeline by the time they were complete.

✪   ✪   ✪

The hard work and quick wit Brad showed throughout the investigation got him the foot in the door that he needed to get to the next step in his career. After a couple of years, he was able to move up to investigations starting in white-collar crimes.

Eventually, he found something that excited him more than the crimes. He discovered the analytics of crime through technology research. Brad loved uncovering facts and formulating leads through undisputable paper trails. Since 1983, he continued to be fascinated by computers, learning more and more about coding/programming as it became more a part of the world. Soon, Brad ended up with a role as one of the first Hi-Tech Crimes Investigation units in the state.

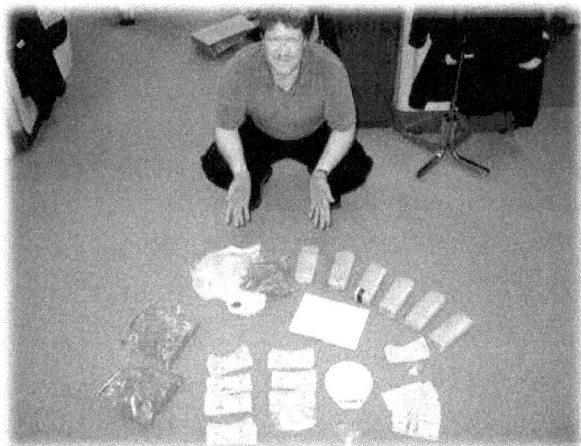

The end of 1999 brought many amazing opportunities for Brad with the fulfillment he was looking for in both his personal and professional life. He worked in conjunction with the Regional Computer Forensics Lab in Kansas City, an amazing team of investigators and computer techies. Together they created protocols for collecting evidence and investigating crimes on this new thing they were calling the Internet.

✪ ✪ ✪

CHAPTER 4

THE DEATH OF OLIVE STUMPP

There is peace in the winter, but it often brings a sense of dark gloom when you are in the middle of the snowy silence. Trees are bare, animals are quiet, people are hidden away from the cold, and the world is bare of the normal vibrancy with blankets of black and white devoid of any sign of life. Maybe the stir craziness of it all was the reason the dead of winter had brought a surge of crimes to the county, but one thing was certain, these weren't just petty crimes but some of the most heinous crimes recorded in the county.

Marvin Stumpp was a bus driver in the Leonardville, Kansas school district. At 0637, on a snowy December morning, Marvin rolled himself out of his warm bed next to his sleeping wife, quickly kissed her forehead, covered her pink floral pajamas with the blanket, and then readied himself for working in the bitter cold of a Kansas winter. Balancing his coffee in one hand while locking the deadbolt to his backdoor with the other, he smiled at the Christmas lights shining through the window of the front door. He was looking forward to the school break starting soon so he could sleep in with his wife.

Marvin crunched through the snow, started the school bus, and waited a few minutes for everything to warm up before he headed out to pick up his kids for the day. Slow and steady, he told himself, but there was no need to fall behind. He needed to be back to pick up Olive by 8:15, so he could take her to work at the bank. He made a few stops while greeting kids along the way. His wife had recently had knee surgery and she was still having a hard time getting around. He did not like her driving on her own to work, but she was excited to get back.

She was often halfway out the door to greet him by the time he got back from the route, her smiling face beaming through the same glass window he smiled through this morning.

When he returned home shortly before 8:15, he glanced into the door window but did not see his wife's beautiful face. He got out of the bus to see if she was almost ready and turned his head against the harsh, stinging wind blowing against his face. He scrunched his face at the shoe prints coming from the field up to the house and then went to unlock the door when he found it already unlocked.

The moment he stepped onto the tile in the mudroom he knew something was wrong. The house was too quiet, considering how far out they lived in the country. Unannounced guests don't usually just show up. His heart started to jump with anxiety, worrying if Olive had fallen.

"Olive," he called out.

The house was still eerily silent with only the hum of the heater in the background. He made his way through the house, looking into the rooms and calling her name, but she was nowhere to be found. Maybe she had to be into work early today and he forgot. Did one of her coworkers take her in?

He rushed to the telephone on the kitchen counter and phoned the bank in town. She would have left a note if her schedule had changed, and he needed to be sure.

"Leonardville Bank," a soft female voice answered. *"Has Olive Stumpp made it work yet by chance,"* Marvin asked. *"No, sir,"* the soft voice replied.

"Are you sure?" he asked, getting more grief-stricken by the second.

"Yes, sir, she is the last person we are waiting on for today." Marvin thanked the soft voice and dropped the phone onto the receiver.

As he turned to go through the house again, his eyes stopped on the basement door, which was not latched all the way. He knew she generally would not go down there by herself since she'd just had knee surgery and stairs were not allowed.

He opened the door and was met by cool, silent darkness, *"Olive?"*.

No reply yet. His eyes were not adjusted to the darkness. Marvin remembered the light overhead and pulled the string.

As he turned on the light he almost fell as he saw his wife in a heap at the bottom of the basement concrete floor, a shadow all around her. Her face didn't look right, and she didn't look like she was breathing. Oh God, what had she done? He thought as he reached her and put his hand over her mouth to see if she was breathing. There was so much blood, he had to get help, and as quickly as he could, he raced back up the concrete stairs, grabbed the phone and dialed 911 on the cold December morning in 1999.

A mellow female voice says into the phone line, *"911, what is your emergency?"*

"Yes, Oh God, Marvin, Marvin Stumpp. I need help, oh please, please, I think my wife fell. I don't know. I don't think she is breathing."

The female voice on the other end of the line is more urgent now, *"Sir, see if you can find a pulse. What is the address there? Where are you now?"*

Marvin Stumpp replied, *"She is in the basement, our home, there's so much blood, oh god, there is too much blood, she isn't breathing. Please hurry."*

Officer Quinton, a senior officer who lived in the North County area, was dispatched to the Stumpp's residence. Officer Quinton was making the rounds that day, driving through the quiet residential streets, marveling at the serenity hiding away in the cold, snowy day. It was a quiet morning in the suburban part of town, and Officer Quinton had just stopped by the drive-thru for a hot coffee to purge the chill seeping into his bones. However, as soon as his turn had arrived in the line of cars, the radio crackled to life with the dispatcher giving the details for the call.

Officer Quinton was familiar with the neighborhood as he was often assigned to work in the small northern cities. He became acquainted with many of the people living there, and it helped him stay up to date with happenings in the area to be prepared and informed. Hearing the address for the Stumpp's, he quickly picked up the pace and sped off towards the farmhouse with the sound of his siren trying to drown his worry about the older couple.

He knew the address as many of the residents often greeted him on the quaint streets early in the morning as Marvin Stumpp was driving the kids to school.

When Officer Quinton reached the house, the ambulance had not yet arrived, and everything seemed too quiet. He could feel something in the air; a sense of loss surrounded the house. He stepped out of the warm patrol car into the frigid winter air and pulled his coat a little tighter with his gloved hands as he walked up to the house. His black work boots crunched through the frozen snow, and the moment he reached the back door, it flew open to an obviously distraught man, his face pale and forehead creased in worry over dark grey eyebrows.

"I think she's dead," Marvin said, his voice cracking.

Officer Quinton watched his face, and the grief was evident in the brown tear-filled eyes. He nodded and let him lead the way.

"It's started just like any other day. I told her countless times not to go downstairs without me there. She had surgery in her knees, and she couldn't get around well on her own." Marvin seemed to be talking to himself, filling the silence by talking about the only thing he could about, the events of that morning.

"She just...she was fine, asleep, when I left. I don't know why she would ever get..., go to the basement." His shoulders shook, and his head hung down.

Wrinkled hands covered his face, as his voice cracked on the last word. The facade he was building, that everything would be fine, cracked as they reached the basement door. Marvin slowly reached out and turned the brass knob to the wooden steps leading to the basement below. The two men walked down the steps one after the other, the stench of blood growing thicker around them the closer they got to the now cold body.

Finally, when they reached the bottom of the stairs, Officer Quinton saw her. Olive Stumpp lay face up surrounded by a pool of crimson blood, and the crack in Marvin's facade deepened and then slipped away as he read the confirmation of his wife's death on the officer's face.

Marvin told Officer Quinton about the morning up until he had dialed 911. *"The next thing I remember is you knocking on the door. I didn't know what else to do. I was just...here..."*

Officer Quinton nodded sympathetically and gently placed his gloved hand on the older gentleman's shoulder for comfort.

He then turned his attention to the reason he was there, the pale, lifeless body on the cold concrete floor. The blood pooling around her had begun to congeal, the smell nauseating, although Officer Quinton showed no sign that it was a bother to him. His face was impassive, minus a sadness sitting right behind the eyes as he swapped out his gloves and crouched down next to her carefully. His gloved hands picked up her pale, rigid wrist, trying to feel for a pulse that had probably been stopped for some time now. He studied the darkened blood and the pale greying color of her face, all indicating that she had probably been lying on the floor for some time and had succumbed to her injuries during her fall.

Officer Quinton stood back up to his full 6 feet, walked solemnly toward Marvin, *"The ambulance is on its way,"* and turned back toward Olive.

She lay on the hard concrete floor. Her legs bent in an unnatural position one under the other that were clad in black stretch pants, the green Christmas sweater now soaked in blood at the back.

"I don't know why she would be down here or why she would be wearing those pants," Marvin mumbled to seemingly no one.

Quinton turned to look at him questioningly. *"What do you mean?"* His dark grey eyebrow raised with curiosity.

"Olive only wears those pants if there's someone at the door. She would never open the door in pajamas." Marvin shook his head in confusion.

While she may have fallen down the stairs, it's possible she may have met someone at the door before it happened. Officer Quinton thought it odd, but there seemed to be no other indication of another person being here that he could see. He knelt next to the body once again and reached for the pen he kept in his shirt pocket. He couldn't do much since he was not an EMT, but he used his pen and tilted her head slightly to get a better look.

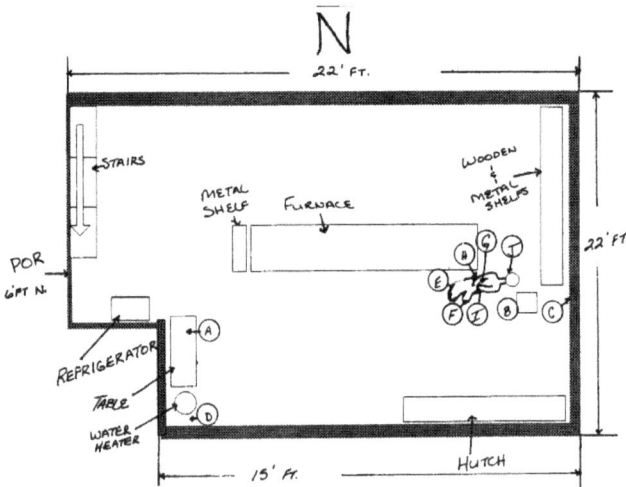

It didn't take long for the house to be swarming with medical team personnel. The sirens echoed into the air as they edged into the driveway tearing away the serenity that comes from a winter morning in the country in despairing darkness. As a second officer arrived to help Officer Quinton guide Marvin, the shock and grief etched into his face, outside to clear the scene for the incoming help.

The medical personnel swarmed around the house, much like flies attracted to the dead. At this point, the death was unattended and accidental, but it was necessary to confirm the cause. Although it seemed like if it was a fall that ended Olive's life, they had to determine if it was under suspicious circumstances.

Marvin sat in the cold, the blanket around him quite useless. To him, it seemed the cold was coming from the inside of him, out. He looked out and although there was a lot of activity around him he saw nothing until the paramedics came out with the stretcher, his wife beneath the crisp white sheet.

"Where are they taking her?" he asked Officer Quinton in a puff of breath.

"To the hospitals for the x-rays. It will give us a preliminary explanation into what happened."

Marvin said nothing, eyes fixated on the ambulance as it drove away from the back door and down the long drive. Officer Quinton quickly asked one of the officers who had shown up on scene to keep an eye on the distraught Marvin and headed inside. He went into the basement and looked around one last time as if it were a crime scene, leaving the hollow, empty space with nothing to suggest it was not an accident. Once everyone had left, he also headed upstairs to see what still needed to be handled.

Officer Quinton departed for Mercy Hospital, leaving an officer with Marvin. He arrived at the hospital shortly after the ambulance and was met by a doctor as he entered the ER to see what they had learned. It was a slow morning in the ER. Normally there were lines of sick people and screaming kids in the waiting room. This time he was met with silence. They were able to move Olive directly into an exam room from the ambulance. A doctor emerged from the room, quickly seeing Officer Quinton working his way through the ER.

"Officer", the doctor called out. *"Are you here for Olive Stumpp? The x-ray showed a bullet lodged in her head."*

Shocked, Officer Quinton called dispatch on the hospital phone. *"Don't let Officer Harlow clear the scene. We have a homicide."*

Thinking it was an accident, everyone at the hospital left the family to deal with their grief and plan funeral arrangements.

Officer Quinton quickly jumped into his Crown Victoria and started sliding on the snow, almost losing control. He told himself to "Calm Down" to regain control and get back to the scene 20 minutes away in the Leonardville countryside.

As the Officer's shoes crunched through the frozen snow, he approached the more senior Officer Harlow. He pulled him aside and explained what was learned at the hospital. Marvin sat dazed on the hood of a patrol car, and Officer Quinton did not want him to overhear this conversation.

"We just got word from the hospital that a bullet was found in her head. How did we miss the evidence of this being a murder scene", he asked awkwardly.

They knew there was no time for arguments since this was now a murder investigation, and everything had changed with the grieving husband Marvin at the top of the suspect list.

They needed to go about this investigation without arousing suspicion until the investigators arrived.

Since Officer Quinton was the first on scene and had already built a rapport with Marvin, they felt he would be more appropriate for Officer Quinton to question him.

He began by asking if they kept any guns in the house, and Marvin led the police to the living room, where he kept a 22 rifle behind the couch. Officer Quinton studied the weapon and then noted the spent shell that was left in the chamber. When he took a quick sniff, there was no evidence it was fired recently. At this point he handed the weapon to Officer Harlow to be cataloged as evidence.

"Alright, Marvin. When you came into the house, did you see anything out of the ordinary? Anything missing? Anything valuable?"

Marvin went from dazed to confused and the lines deepened above his dark-colored eyebrows. *"I...no...why? I thought Olive fell. What's going on?"* His suspicion grew as the seconds passed.

"We need to be sure of what happened which is why we're running through every possible scenario," Officer Quinton said, trying to put Marvin's mind at ease.

Marvin calmed down until he suddenly looked up at the increasing activity at the doorway. Rushing towards the doorway, he screamed, "STOP!"

Immediately everyone froze, eyes turning to Marvin in curiosity as he scrambled across the driveway. Marvin turned to Officer Quinton and explained the footprints he had seen earlier this morning. He led the officer over to the unknown footprints with Detective Rhino, who had just arrived.

"They were over there," he said, pointing to the area that led to the tree line on the edge of the property. Clearly, there were fresh prints in the snow, the cold weather and overcast sky keeping them frozen in place.

Marvin then walked back through the house, where once again, they repeated the questions about the missing items. Marvin tried to think about it but the chaos of the day and not knowing what happened to Olive was taking its toll. The detective allowed him time, letting him walk from room to room to look until finally, he saw that one of his drawers was open. He rushed over to it and found that his old brown wallet was not in there.

"What was in there?" Detective Rhino asked, scribbling on his notepad.

"There might be about $100 in there, and a second wallet had two $2 bills inside. It was lying open in the drawer," Marvin said.

The detective nodded, and the team turned their attention back to the scene of the murder. With the newfound knowledge of a bullet wound, the team was now even more thorough. The dimness of the basement made it difficult. The walls were lined with shelves, each row filled with jars or cans of preserved food to weather out a storm that was anticipated with the hysteria of Y2K in the near future.

Detective Rhino, the department CSI, had taken over the crime scene now, and until the autopsy reports were released, they would have to deal with what information they had. He returned to where the body was found and made notes for the report he would need to file later.

"Mrs. Stumpp was laying with her feet nearest to the steps coming down into the basement as if facing the steps when she fell." Detective Rhino wrote this information down as he made notes. He then looked around the area and located an old wooden sink and table to the right of the stairs that had quite a few items on it. There he found a shell casing for a 9mm weapon. A diligent search of the dimly lit, cluttered basement located a second shell casing that would have been within 2 feet of Olive's head if she was still there. The wall across the flight of stairs sported a mark about four and a half feet high that was consistent with a ricochet mark. Detectives were photographing, examining, and noting every minute detail of the crime scene, including the footprints outside

that had been frozen into a perfect mold due to the dropping arctic freezing temperatures.

One of the detectives knelt next to the print and pushed his glasses up the bridge of his nose as he studied the casting. Some of the elements of the footprint had been lost, which would have provided ample information about the suspect. Regardless, there were still aspects of the shoes that seemed to catch the detective's attention and he called Detective Rhino to go over the details of the footprint with him.

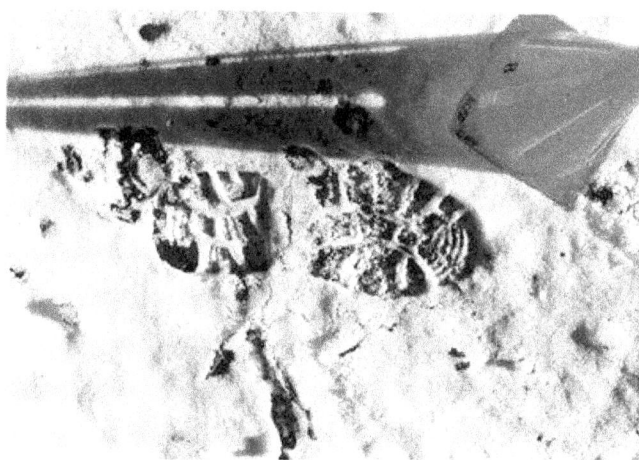

They knelt next to one another and looked at the footprint as the detective explained, *"It looks like a hiking-type boot, and if you look there..."* he said, pointing to the center of the print. *"...There*

is a little banner that had something written on it, but I can't make out anything".

Just like at the dentist when you get your teeth molded, the detectives used dental molding to cast the print in the decaying snow as the heat of the day started to creep up on them. With the casting set, they were able to take a closer look at the banner on the print.

"Look! It has a number 8 next to it."

Detective Rhino leaned in, looking closer at the print of the shoe, he recognized the print from somewhere, but he just could not quite place where. Much later in the investigation, a detailed vendor search revealed that the boot was unique. The detectives went from store to store looking for the tread pattern and banner to match the boot print. Size 8 was small. Were they looking for a woman or a kid?

Finally, the search yielded an answer, the boot was a Northwest Territories brand boot distributed by K-Mart, but when was it sold, and who purchased it? There is only one K-Mart in the area but with no idea of when the boots were sold, the search through the store records could take forever, and video surveillance is likely to be false too.

Detectives would later use this mold to locate a sample pair of the boots. They would show the mold to prospective witnesses and make posters asking the public to share information if they knew of someone who wore a similar boot.

At the scene, the detectives made the necessary arrangements and finished their work collecting the evidence not knowing what was important at this point of the investigation. Detective Rhino stood and looked around the canvas, the line of yellow police tape flapping noisily in the crisp winter wind, we need to get busy, he exclaimed.

Detectives discovered someone had entered the Stumpp property and had apparently walked north along a small row of trees. The individual then paced back and forth behind the Stumpp propane tank, located just east of the house.

Detective Rhino made his way over to the nearly 6- foot-high tank and looked down at the tracks continuing to the south door. The marks appeared to be partially on the porch before moving down and around to the west side of the house, ending at the north entrance. Upon exiting the north door, the tracks proceeded north out of the yard across a snow-covered field.

Detective Rhino looked around at the snow falling again in fat silent flakes through the grey and dreary sky. He knew they needed to trace the movements before the snow covered the tracks and ruined them from further evidence. They needed to canvas the area immediately. Detective Rhino gathered his team to follow the path out through the field.

The ominous feelings throughout the day seemed to continue as they worked their way in the frigid air. The people working on the case had felt a fierce protective urge for their families back home, and whether it was the chill of the winter or the fear of this unknown man on the loose, they just didn't know. The unknowns of the case had incited an anxious fear with increased motivation to keep the community safe.

The officers continued following the path of footprints, crossing through tree lines, fences, through bushes, and faces red from the freezing wind. At one point, the tracks changed direction. The suspect had begun walking west from Barton Road, traveling through the field by the nursing home, and then the footprints broke off at Alembic Road.

Mid-morning, there was significantly more traffic mixed with the roar of the engines driving by. The wind picked up force resounding over the area. The police noticed the tracks became muddled but they could follow the distinctive pattern through several fields and ended up on the east side of town by the golf club. Unfortunately, the tracks were no longer discernible to follow.

"All right, start canvassing the area. I need you to locate anyone who has any information to help us discern a direction in the investigation. Look for clues, suspicious activity, ask around the areas we've tracked," Detective Rhino barked the orders, and the team nodded and headed out.

CHAPTER 5

FOLLOWING THE TRACKS

Leonardville was a small town where people gossiped and spread more rumors than facts. This was a pressing issue with the investigation, especially since most of the gossip made the police run around in circles and sometimes ended with false suspects apprehended.

At the beginning of the investigation, it was evident that Marvin was the lead suspect. Although his alibi checked out, they still couldn't completely rule him out. The main questions circulating through the department were about his motive and how the murder would have occurred. The method was straightforward as determined through the coroner's reports, but the motive was still unclear.

Everyone who was familiar with the couple said the same thing: they lived a quiet life. Olive was a well-respected member of the community who worked at the bank for decades, helping the locals keep their homes and businesses going. That meant there was no need for her to be targeted in a murder unless she refused someone a loan.

Detective Rhino made notes with ongoing questions on a whiteboard and circled back every few days with updates. However, the outcomes were always the same. As Olive's background was cleared, the questions moved toward Marvin. There was no doubt that Marvin was the anti-social, typical country boy who worked in the fields for years. He retired and drove a school bus just to keep himself busy.

As the officers continued the investigation surrounding Marvin, maintaining him as the primary suspect, the question that continued to play in their minds was whether or not Marvin was actually leading a double life. It seemed possible, but again, no evidence suggested it. None that the officers could find anyway.

It was yet another dark morning in the small town when during another visit around the neighborhood, one of the residents living in the vicinity of Olive and Marvin's house stopped Officer Harlow. He was a gangly man who said that he would often pass by the Stumpp residence on his way to play golf.

"Sir, if you could tell us what you know…", Officer Harlow asked, keeping him on track.

He didn't think the information he was going to receive would be relevant, but it was his job to make a note of whatever information he could find.

As the chill of the winter morning intensified, the resident's next words sparked the fire of interest.

"I believe, officer, that you should be looking into Marvin, and not some random stranger," the man said, his voice laced with secrecy.

Officer Harlow noted it with feigned interest, knowing it was just what they were doing.

"Okay, sir. Can you tell me why you think that?" he further inquired, thinking it would come down to a long grudge the two might have shared.

"Well, Marvin has an eye for the girls. Marvin would disappear for days at a time to Nebraska", the man said, but before he could elaborate, his

wife appeared and was scared at the sight of the police.

It took a while until the realization dawned on her that Officer Harlow was just investigating the murder. In general, townspeople wanted to stay far from cases to keep themselves safe from involvement. The resident couldn't elaborate more with his wife listening, but before leaving, he said that the police should look at Marvin's phone records.

Furlow, the resident, was officially a suspect, especially considering he was the only one to directly talk to the police about Marvin's possible unfaithfulness to his late wife. He mentioned, seemingly annoyed that he had seen Marvin's school bus parked west of his house facing south many times.

"People are creatures of habit," he said before going on a rant about how much it bothered him that the bus was parked northbound, facing east of the house on the day of the homicide.

And just like that, the quiet town had come alive with the horror of Olive's death. As the investigations continued, more of the city's secrets rose from the ashes, but none of them seemed critical to the investigation. Officer Harlow immediately called up the station and informed them of the updates he had received.

The resident's words didn't seem useless. After all, the investigators themselves had doubts about Marvin. There was something about his quiet demeanor that didn't sit well with the initial investigators. Once Officer Harlow's input was received, it was evident that they had to call Marvin in for a polygraph test.

The motion was set in place, and an examiner was called in from the KBI, Kansas Bureau of Investigations. Officer Quinton was sent to pick up Marvin, and he reluctantly agreed. While Officer Quinton was dedicated to his work, he often had trouble confronting people he knew, including escorting them into the station.

As Officer Quinton drove to Marvin's house, he couldn't shake the immense coldness that seeped into his bones. An ominous cloud of death loomed all over the house; the tree on their front porch was dying from a lack of care that Olive had provided. The Christmas lights hung loosely around it, a glimpse of a life that had once lit up the house.

Officer Quinton stepped out of his car and walked up to the door, where Marvin was ready to leave to get groceries. He turned around and met the seriousness of Officer Quinton's eyes

"Is there an update?", he asked, seemingly hopeful.

"Not yet, but we would like you to come down to the station and relate the incident one more time for us. We need to be sure we have a note of every detail", Officer Quinton said.

A flash of understanding crossed Marvin's face, and he nodded. The two of them walked to the car, their footsteps crunching on the snow, and then drove off.

"You know you're wasting time looking into me when the real killer is out there," Marvin said after a couple of minutes of silence. Officer Quinton looked in his rearview mirror then turned back to the road, choosing not to respond.

Officer Rhino was waiting at the station and took Marvin in for the interview. After going through his story a few more times for consistency, Marvin was informed he would be taking a polygraph test. Marvin nodded, silently agreeing to it. He sat in a room with nothing but a large steel desk in the middle and a large mirror in front of him. He looked at his reflection with the lines that crossed his face, making him look so much older than he was.

The interview didn't take too long to start once the KBI examiner walked in with his machine. The examiner, in his 60's, had seasoned experience with suspects undergoing investigation. He kept up his poker face, ensuring that Marvin knew he was unmoved by the story being presented.

By now, Marvin was on edge. The polygraph exam was a brutal process when done correctly. It was the examiner's duty to elevate the test subject's anxiety level to create a baseline. It was only after that they could begin the examination and hope to see a rise in the physiological signs of stress above the baseline from the questions asked. Often, the anxiety alone could produce false-positive results, or more commonly, inconclusive results reported as lies.

Marvin's future and his testimony were on the edge of the precipice. As a result, once the test was over, the examiner was left with an inconclusive result.

"Do you think he's responsible for her death?" Officer Rhino asked him when he stepped outside and closed the door.

"Perhaps. I do believe that he is somehow responsible. I don't know how," the examiner said.

"Well, alright. Thank you for your time." "Good luck," the examiner said as he walked towards the exit.

Little did the RCPD know, the interview was the beginning of a downward spiral of trust from the Stumpp family. There was no more reason left to detain Marvin, and so he was sent home.

With Marvin set aside, the investigation was then turned towards the local residents. The officers went back to the whiteboard to refresh their stances and spent their time trying to reel back to the crime scene. Finally, Officer Quinton stepped up and said he had a suspect in mind that he preferred to look into.

"Who?" Officer Rhino inquired.

"Daniel Thatcher. When we were following the trail on the day of the murder, it led to the area where he lived. Daniel is known for his...let's

say, troublesome ways. He was recently caught for starting a bar fight."

"Alright. You look into him and get me an update," Officer Rhino said. Quinton nodded, grabbed his cap, and went on his way.

Officer Quinton knew Daniel Thatcher was a handful and wouldn't be interested in any interviews for at least a few days until the freshness of the bar fight died down. A couple of days later, Officer Quinton made his way down the dark, deserted road towards an even darker house with a single light bulb hanging on the porch. He knocked on the door, and after a while, a woman opened up.

"Yes?", she said, hugging her cardigan close.

"Hello, my name is Officer Quinton. I'd like to have a few words with Daniel Thatcher."

"Oh. Daniel has been working a lot of night shifts and hasn't returned home yet," she said.

Officer Quinton thought about it. He already had an excuse ready in case something like this happened. Daniel was known to wear hiking boots, which he hoped had the size stamped in the sole, like the boot prints found in the snow.

"Would you mind if I see his room?", he asked. Knowing Officer Quinton was known around town. Daniel's mother didn't hesitate and opened the door wide for him.

"Is he in any trouble? What did he do now?", she asked, concerned.

"Nothing to be too concerned about, ma'am. Don't worry," he said reassuringly.

"Well, alright. His room is right down the hall to the left," she said.

Daniel's room was quite a mess. His unmade bed had an empty bowl on it, and his dresser was in disarray. Right by the door, however, were his shoes. Officer Quinton bent low and carefully examined the boots. Immediately, he found the shoes sitting there atop a rack. With a pen in hand, Officer Quinton took a look at it.

"Are these the only boots Daniel owns?" he asked.

"Yes, they are. He wears nice shoes & slacks to work," she replied.

Officer Quinton could feel his heart racing as he felt the excitement of stumbling upon a lead.

There, on the inside of the boot, was written "Size 8," and there was evidence of mud on the soles. However, much to his disappointment, as he scraped away the mud, he noted that the bottom was not stamped with the "8" and the tread was not the same. Disappointed, he placed the boot back and stood up.

"Well, thank you for your time, Mrs. Thatcher," he said, and the woman walked him to the door. As soon as he stepped outside, he felt the cold on his face, and the disappointment crept into him for going back to square one.

The vital 48 hours had passed, and fewer leads were coming in. Everything seemed to be entirely still. By then, detective Lufkin had decided to turn towards the paper trail in an attempt to find leads. He investigated the customers at the bank, still wondering if the motive was to rob the bank.

They looked at all the transactions leading up to the date of the murder and even ran backgrounds on the customers with loans. Background checks were made for phone calls incoming and outgoing to the bank and the Stumpp's personal calls all turned up nothing. They failed to find a single person who had suspicious activity.

The media had now reached the station, and journalists were clinging on to any updates. To share information quickly to the media, a press conference was held. The Chief of Police sat behind a mic with Officer Quinton beside him and a few detectives from the scene. Journalists sat in the audience, taking notes. Now and then, a flash would go off. Bright white light lit up the room.

"All we know right now is that on December 15th, 1999 at approximately 08:30, Riley County Police Department received a 911 call from Marvin Stumpp of Barton Road. Mr. Stumpp had returned home from work and found his wife, Mrs. Olive Stumpp, deceased."

"Mrs. Stumpp died a violent death, and it is being investigated as a homicide. Anyone with any information is requested to contact the Riley County Police Department. We will not be entertaining any further questions. Thank you," The Chief cut the questions off and stood up along with the other investigators leaving them only with his prepared statement.

The crowd erupted with questions, each of them rushing to the police to get some answers.

However, the team of investigators quickly left the room following their queue from the Chief.

It wasn't long after that that the KBI website posted a KBI reward of $1,000 for information leading to an arrest. Mrs. Stumpp's family posted a $5,000 reward for information, which eventually would lead to the conviction of the person responsible for the murder.

The RCPD station had suddenly become much more active. The entire department came alive with the ringing of the telephones. Day after day, calls came in mentioning sights of people seen wearing Northwest Territory Hiking boots and neighbors suspecting neighbors of having some involvement with the murder. It further jeopardized the investigation and led them towards more dead ends. The more the officers tried to understand the case, the more they came up with loose ends and wild speculative stories.

Meanwhile, neighbors came up and accused Marvin of having an affair with a woman in Nebraska. It only presented the police with more motives for murder. However, the more they looked into it, the more information they failed to receive. Eventually, it only led them to have even less direct connections to the actual murder.

The police department was left with immense hopelessness when it came to the murder. Too much time had passed, and there was nothing to show for it. They did come across their fair share of suspects. But in the end, they all turned out to be false.

While one of the suspects reported to the police that Mr. McDonald, the town's elite, might be behind the murder because of Olive uncovering his money laundering and other illegal activities, another claimed her boss might have something to do with it. Her boss was an owner of a café who often bragged about already committing two murders, thereby placing himself under keen observation.

The person in question was Mr. Brighton, who was often seen as vindictive and strange by everyone who passed him. He had an aura of arrogance, much like his wife. However, to everyone's disappointment, the lead later went cold with no evidence found that might have linked Mr. Brighton to the Stumpp murder, or any other murder.

Just like that, several suspects came forward, pushing the investigation along but ending in nothing. Just as the police department thought of closing a case that had begun to go cold, another suspect came forward. Now, this one was different. It immediately grabbed their attention.

Jimmy Niles was a convicted felon who was on his parole the day it happened. Upon further investigation, it became clear that he was within the vicinity of the crime scene. A ray of hope finally spread in the department. It was an opportunity that opened up a way to show the town that the police were, in fact, doing the best they could and still working up new leads.

The RCPD had begun facing backlash for their 'incompetence' to get someone in custody from the residents of the town. The end of the New Year brought about new hope for the department.

Jimmy was a rowdy-looking man but otherwise couldn't be recognized as a felon. He did hold a certain air of mystery. Detective Ryan and Detective Fleck were responsible for taking care of this investigation, as it had now been categorized as a Cold Case. So he had deemed it best to carry out a CVSA, Computerized Voice Stress Analysis, which was similar to the polygraph.

However, the examiner conducting the interview noticed that Jimmy remained on edge. His stress was elevated, and he underwent partial blocking of the graphs, thereby making the results unreliable. Detective Ryan refused to take this as a defeat and decided to carry out a polygraph interview.

Jimmy Niles later agreed to take a polygraph test to show the police that he was in no way involved with the murder. He had gone as far as also telling the police that the perpetrator should be given the death penalty.

Being a burglar, he claimed that he had never resorted to violence, and it was a heinous accusation leveled on him.

Jimmy Niles was later dragged through the process for longer than the rest of the suspects because Detective Ryan and Fleck were convinced that he was somehow involved. He gave off an aura that prevented them from trusting him.

Eventually, however, it turned out that they had nothing else to keep Niles in custody, and so had to let him go. They were back without a lead, and the case was now dying out, just as the chill of winter died down through the little town.

✪ ✪ ✪

2002 was just around the corner. Merriment spread with the start of Christmas, red and white filling up every corner of the otherwise bleak police department. The Christmas party included music, drinks, the County Attorney, and an assistant county attorney. While snowflakes covered the streets and glazed over the windows, the celebrations commenced, to last through the night.

Members of the police department had walked into Detective's Rhino's country home, yielding boxes wrapped in brightly colored papers and ribbons. A tree sat in the corner, its ornaments glistening in the bright lights that lit up the festivities. Everyone enjoyed swapping inexpensive white elephant gifts and stories with their loved ones offering a glimpse of what their job was like while on duty, often with strings of laughter.

However, as the night went on and the energy began to die down ever so slowly, the consumption of alcohol led to conversations about Olive Stumpp, the case that forever tainted the RCPD in a dark picture amongst the townsfolk. The residents had nearly lost faith in the police department, especially after Marvin was eliminated as a suspect and they were not able to find another viable suspect for three years.

Two detectives were still working on the case, and both were adamant about convicting Jimmy Niles.

However, the county attorneys weren't left in the dark when it came to the case. They were also aware of how the detectives had prepared an affidavit for the arrest of Jimmy Niles. However, no matter how much they pushed for it, the attorneys were still reluctant to take the warrant to the judge. As the night came to an end, the detectives had to accept the current fate of the case.

Due to the lack of direct witnesses and warrants, they had to admit that the case was now cold. One of the main reasons was the missing gun, boots, or direct evidence, which prevented the cops from placing Niles at the scene of the crime. Little did they know, the loopholes in their investigation would be uncovered soon, bringing the lingering mystery to light.

CHAPTER 6

HAUNTING CRIMES

During the time of the Olive Stumpp homicide, Officer Brad White was busy with his own investigations. He would spend his time tracking down culprits and using his expertise in intelligence gathering, computers, and technology to define his niche for the department.

The years continued to pass, and investigators chased down every lead from the Stumpp homicide with the case getting more cold as time went on.

While the chill of death lingered around the small town, the rumors of the case going cold traveled through the halls of the station. It was a sore topic in the investigation division of the department. In 2001 after White was promoted to the Investigations Division, he was assigned as the White-Collar Crimes Detective to take up the financial and complex crimes. He went straight to business and began developing the Hi-Tech Crime Unit with his computer programming skills. There was not much to work with since the internet was new, there was no budget for this, and the idea of collecting evidence from electronics was absurd. Officer White started by collecting computers from drug seizures, and pieced together a forensic computer, air-gapped from the rest of the world to process the evidence. Air gapped is a security measure in which computers, computer systems, or networks are not connected in any way to any other devices or networks. This is used in instances requiring airtight security without the risk of compromise or disaster.

Then some policies and protocols needed to be created to create a standard. Luckily there were a lot of geeks in law enforcement working hand in hand with the RCFL (Regional Computer Forensic Lab) FBI in Kansas City. Riley County now had a working Hi-Tech Crime Unit too.

As unexpected as things go, a case had just come in which would pull Det. White away from his normal Hi-Tech crimes. The Chief called Det. White into his office, where he had just hung up the phone with the City Manager. A member of the founding families of Manhattan, KS, was working as the superintendent of the Parks & Recreation. The superintendent was having issues with funds going missing from his department. The problem was that the superintendent didn't report it. The report came from an intern working in the finance department, noting inconsistent deposits.

The detectives dropped by the Parks & Recreation Office in the earliest hours when the silence of sheer emptiness engulfed the office. Detective White, along with his colleagues were well-versed in what he had to do, and the plan was very well in check. Once they entered the building, only the faint light of their flashlights lit up the entire room. They looked around. The grey carpeted flooring helped to mask the sounds of the steps.

The guard stood posted as Detective White entered the room, helping him set up his things. The team went over to the attic of a staff member's office building and set up covert cameras in the vents. They were aimed at a dropbox where the crews would drop funds from the days' activities, an overall view of the office, and another on the door to make a positive ID.

Finally, the darkness gave way to a faint red light, and the team knew it was time. They didn't know what to expect, but whatever it was, they didn't expect this.

Without realizing it, they had managed to open a can of worms. Once they went back to the station and logged into the CCTV camera, the black and white screen buzzed, and then the pixelated image came into view. After only two days of activities, it was not difficult to make out what was going on.

In the video, they saw the superintendent opening the drop location. Instead of counting the money for accuracy and making the deposits, he was putting a fair amount of the undocumented funds into his pockets. Detective White watched, intrigued. He knew he needed to investigate the superintendent further before making the big reveal.

He spent hours going through files, pictures, and documentation about him, and finally, it was uncovered that there was a gambling scam that took place in the city. He discovered that the city employees were betting on fantasy football, not only on company time but with city money.

The more Detective White dug into the files, the more things he uncovered of the day-to-day operations of the City Parks & Recreation Department. His discoveries made him understand that this wasn't anything new, it had been going on for years, unfortunately. Detective White was excellent at his work, but he knew he wasn't an accounting expert.

In order to truly understand what was happening, he needed to gain the help of the City Finance Office. He didn't waste time calling them up. He immediately briefed the office with as much detail as was necessary. Side by side, they pieced together the events.

The projected earnings should have been deposited, and the missing totals hit six figures. Detective White was excited about how close he was to uncover the truth. The days had suddenly gone longer while only one group stayed on the murder investigation.

One morning when Detective White woke up, he decided it was finally time to interview the suspect. Detective White was determined to end this.

It was a momentous day, and he was instructed to wear a suit and tie, which was in contrast to his everyday jeans and t-shirt attire. As soon as he dressed, he called up the Chief of Police and the Mayor as he received the update. They would both be overseeing the interview through the observation monitor. He had walked into the station, prepped and ready.

There was an air of anticipation, and as soon as he entered, he could feel the tense pull on his muscles. Once he entered the interrogation room, with white walls all around him, he knew it was time to do his best. He managed to lay out the entire crime timeline for the gallery and suspect who then provided a remorseful confession about what he could remember doing over the years.

Unfortunately, the superintendent had nothing to show for all the money he had taken other than living lavishly with his friends. He was best known for being the voice of the Kansas State Wildcats as a commentator for the stadium and local radio. That is all over now. One video had effectively brought an end to his career. However, solving this case had served as a win for Detective White.

Brad White's success in this particular case had quickly moved him from white-collar crimes back into narcotics. This was when he was assigned to a task force for the DEA Mobile Enforcement Task Force to gather intelligence for a year.

Officer White spent his time chasing cocaine distributions all over the state and trained with SCAT (Special Community Action Team) units in Wichita, Topeka, and Kansas City. His role transformed into a position as a Major Crimes Investigator. All these roles helped pave the way in a positive direction for Detective White. He became part of the teams that created and led the Clandestine Lab Intervention Team (METH Labs), the underwater recovery team, and the Hi-Tech Crimes Unit.

The team allowed them to be a part of almost every major homicide, drug case, assault, robbery, and investigations concerning Internet Crimes Against Children. Brad was investigating the worst crimes society had to offer.

Detective White's evidence collection methods for Hi-Tech crimes developed over the years, yielding him a 98% conviction ranking for cases based on his evidence and investigations. The team was often assigned cold cases, and Brad was a part of all of it.

His first case came immediately. It was a missing person presumed dead from a drug deal in the 1970s. Detective White felt hopeless even though he slowly gained traction. The witnesses were mostly dead, or they just couldn't remember anything to add to the case file.

The Investigation Team was an integral part of his growth, and it was through them that he was able to develop his skill in interview techniques. Witnesses said that he had a very Colombo interview style, which meant that he would act as if he knew nothing and needed their help to understand even the simplest of details about the crime. Often, he played the role of the Good Cop, because Bad Cop felt so unnatural and forced, which came off as ungenuine.

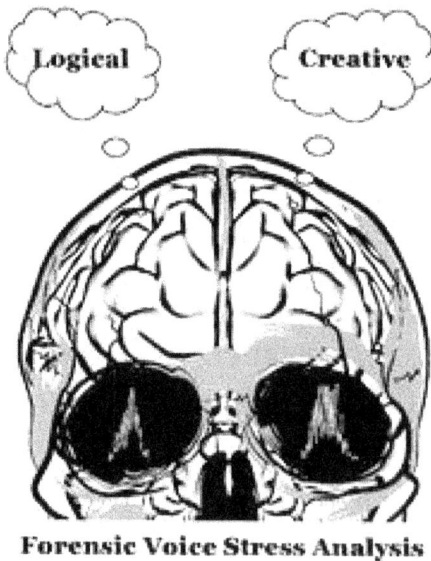

Forensic Voice Stress Analysis

Time passed and his training progressed further as he learned the art of Voice Stress Analysis, a tool used to analyze voice recordings and determine if the subjects were being truthful in their answers. This technology sparked Brad's interest since it was mainly a computer algorithm developed in the 60s to screen soldiers under stress to determine their ability to continue the fight.

The VSA technology was dormant until the 80s, when it got a second look as a tool to help determine truth like a polygraph. This technology differed as it mainly worked off the subconscious responses derived from the autonomic thought process of formulating a lie in the creative part of your brain, rather than the physiological reactions received from direct questions that are measured in a polygraph.

While Detective White was beginning to see a significant uptick in his career, this moment was when he also learned the harsh reality of law enforcement. With great responsibility came grim reality. People on the streets didn't like the police because they only saw the bad associated with their interactions.

The police were always under observation as they were known to only look out only for themselves, their promotions, or how they appeared to the public. The ending of police work was always dark. Many faced early death or no life outside of law enforcement if they made it to retirement. This life was hard on marriages.

✪ ✪ ✪

Then the day we will never forget, September 11, 2001 happened.

The day began like any other morning. The detectives just finished the morning brief of the happenings of patrol the previous night and dispersed to their respective cubicles.

Suddenly at 8:45 am, the tone of the day was shifted forever when Captain Dubbs yelled out from his office. He had been watching TV, and a plane had just hit the twin towers in New York.

A few detectives huddled around his doorway to see the little TV in the corner, then it happened.

9:03 am, a second plane struck the second twin tower, and the mood went from a tragedy to a terrorist attack. All investigative work seemed to stop and the big screen in the briefing room was the main focus of attention. Reporter after reporter speculated on the event on a continuous loop. Graphic slow-motion collisions with the towers, and desperate victims jumping to their death filled the airways to be analyzed.

By the end of the day a sense of panic had set in with all patrol officers on a heightened alert. By the time the third plane hit the pentagon, and a fourth plane full of historic warriors took down the plane heading for the capitol building, the United States was at war with an unknown enemy.

The days following the devastating attack Detective White was assigned to investigate price gouging at the gas stations and other emergency service suppliers. As mundane as it was, he found himself in familiar territory building a database of potential Muslim radicals living in and around Riley County.

The FBI quickly formed a Joint Terrorism Task Force (JTTF) with Det. White goes door to door in the Muslim communities around the college campus following up on tips of suspicious behavior. In hindsight, it was a modern-day witch hunt as patriotic fear of Muslims in general escalated with the attack associated with a Taliban terrorist organization in Afghanistan.

A Muslim basketball player from Kansas State University on injury status was involved in a domestic violence issue with his girlfriend advancing him into the spotlight. Although a young adult, he was well connected in the Muslim community. The FBI decided to use him as an informant to identify those who were developing radical viewpoints and plotting anti-American violence.

The United States started retaliation against those involved in the attack. TV news was focused on the video from bombers, jet fighters, and helicopters as they destroyed their targeted areas with pinpoint precision.

The Muslim communities started their own celebrations. The Muslim informant was capturing video of parties where they gathered showing a drinking game. Every time the TV news had an American or soldier in Afghanistan beheaded, they would take a shot.

"The world will never be the same", said Agent Miller from the FBI, "but we must do our part to protect those we love and serve from themselves, as much as the enemy."

On Sep. 11th, 2,763 lives were taken to expose the vulnerabilities of the United States of America 343 firefighters and 71 police officers were among those rushing into the danger.

✪   ✪   ✪

Most of 2001 was full of advancements for Det. White as he established himself as a unique type of investigator. Unknown to him he was about to be hit with yet another tragedy as the year came to an end. Once again, the darkness of December slowly made its way towards his old department & colleagues at JCPD.

An officer, Officer Alex, responded to a domestic disturbance call. Like Smokey, Officer Alex was a great friend of Brad, and they often met up at family barbecues while speaking German with his wife. Little did they know the friendship was going to come to a bitter end.

It was the beginning of December, in the early hours of the day. He had responded to the scene where a man had opened up the door and was later identified as the boyfriend of the woman who had called for help.

Officer Alex was responsible for the two children trapped inside the house while his partner stood as a backup in the event the suspect fled the scene. The ice on a winter morning had only begun to form, and the darkness had only started to subside. Officer Alex approached the building cautiously walking inside, armed and ready.

"Open up! Police!" he called out as he knocked loudly on the door. Instead, he was met with shuffling of feet and the whimpering of children.

Officer Alex turned back to face his partner, who had nodded at him to continue. Slowly, he moved in front of the door with his gun in his hands, then quickly shoved the door with his shoulder in an attempt to force it open.

Right after the first hit, the door opened, and the loud wails of children echoed in the building. It took a mere second for Officer Alex to see the boyfriend before the fatal bullet embedded itself onto his chest, instantly leaving him shocked, then lifeless.

"Officer down! I repeat, Officer down! I request backup!", his partner called in to the radio and rushed after the suspect, who had successfully locked himself in one of the rooms.

Not long after, another gunshot was heard, making the kids scream louder in the other room. Once Officer Alex's partner broke down the bathroom door, he discovered the suspect had killed himself in fear of the repercussions of Officer Alex's death.

The two children were unarmed. However, the gloomy cloud of death hung heavy in the air.

Once the funeral took place, Detective White realized how close death truly was as he cherished what good moments he had left of his friend. Before he knew it the year had passed, and soon the next year was coming to a close as well.

It was November of 2002 when Detective White was contacted for a homicide in Riley, Kansas. Like every other case White didn't think much about it, but something about the case felt threatening. He felt on edge and without knowing why.

RIP "Alex" End of Watch: 12/3/2001

Little did he know this case would be one of those which would haunt him forever. It all began when a call was made to the RCPD as a mentally unstable woman spoke to her caseworker about wanting to end her life. The caseworker had called up for assistance, mentioning that the woman had two children, and had recently purchased a gun as well.

As soon as the call had arrived, officers were dispatched to check on the women. When the first officer arrived and got out of his vehicle, he walked up to the porch covered with glistening white snow. As he raised his hand to ring the bell, a loud gunshot rang out from inside.

The officer was not informed there were children inside the house, and he rushed to the car to call for backup since portable radios didn't work well this far out in the country. Suddenly, a second and third gunshot rang out. He didn't know if it was the chill of the winter or the gunshot, but he felt the cold hit his bones.

When he could finally connect the call for a backup, it would take them at least 15-20 minutes to respond. The responding SWAT officers rushed inside, but one glimpse their hearts fell to pieces, and they rushed back out as white as snow outside, blanketing the still air.

They could hardly articulate a reply when the detectives arrived.

Once the forensic team made the entry, they were greeted with a horrific scene. All they could see was red, and it was enough to send some of the officers outside nauseated by the sight they just witnessed to throw up in the bushes. In all the years of their work, there was not a single incident they faced half as terrifying as what they had seen. Detective White was asked to document the scene and collect evidence with the CSI investigator Rhino.

None of the officers had ever experienced a site quite as horrific as what they had seen. Officer White wasn't informed of the details but agreed nonetheless to assist the CSI team. He made his way to the house on what he thought was a cheery morning, with no hint of the doom that awaited him in the house of death.

When he parked his car outside the house, all Officer White could see was a swarm of blue and black cars, the red and blue lights reflecting off the patches of crystal white snow. A grim expression was on everyone's faces, the color drained. Detective White could sense the strain that pulled on the atmosphere. As soon as he stepped out of the car, he was handed a mask and gloves from an officer. Detective White thanked him as he looked up and he saw the dread in his eye.

"It's bad. It's really bad. You're on your own. I'm not going back in," he said and walked away.

Detective White looked after him for a while, then focused his attention on the door. When he entered the trailer, he felt the musty air and the stench of blood.

The CSI investigator stood in the living room with the flash of the camera going off. Detective White walked up to him and didn't even call him when the investigator turned around and handed him the camera.

"I'll take the notes as we walk through the initial documentation," he said, blocking Detective White's view of the bodies on the sofa. He began walking towards the back room, his body stiff with every movement.

"That's the room," he said with a cold voice. Detective White looked at it and slowly peered

inside. He had to fight the tears welling into his eyes. All he could see was the pink unicorn bed sheets and a tiny body on top of it.

Crimson red blood was splattered all over the bed and the walls. Slowly, Detective White walked further inside, his heart beating fast in his chest. A little girl lay lifeless on the bed; her innocent face turned towards the wall. The girl was about the same age as Detective White's oldest daughter, which made this even more difficult. While the girl had been shot in the back, the scene was still quite messy.

"That's what a large caliber will do at close range," Detective Rhino said. He walked in and carefully inspected the body.

Detective White fought the urge to cover up the body; the little girl looked so innocent. It made his mind scream with questions, crying to get out. Nonetheless, he had a job to do and a responsibility to get what information he could for the case. He took a deep breath.

"I got this, don't worry," he told Rhino and began taking pictures, fighting the urge to scream and throw up. He made sure he documented all the details, allowing every minute detail of the little girl's crime scene to be noted.

Once he was done, he and Detective Rhino went through the remainder of the back rooms documenting their condition and measurements until he stopped in the hallway. He didn't know that the little girl's bedroom was not even close to the worst scene. He was about to find out more very soon.

"Are you ready?", Detective Rhino asked, looking him dead in the eyes.

Slowly, Brad nodded, bracing himself for the worst. Regardless of how many tragedies he had seen, none of them compared to what he was about to witness.

Detective White could feel the dread; he didn't want to continue, but he had to.

"This isn't just a tragedy; it is what nightmares are made of", Detective Rhino said to himself, although Brad heard the words. He studied the officer's movements and the reluctance in his steps. They had now reached the back door by the bedrooms of the trailer. Rhino paused again, then stepped outside.

"What are you not telling me? Do I know them?", Brad asked, the dread reaching all over his body. Detective Rhino had now turned completely pale.

"I don't think so, but it is bad, really bad", he repeated.

✪ ✪ ✪

Brad sat in his car trying to get in control of his senses, but all he could do now was feel the bile churning in his stomach and his heart quickly beating after viewing the aftereffects of a brutal crime.

The worst of humanity became visible to him. He gripped the steering wheel tighter but couldn't erase the images from his head. His mind kept traveling back to when he had walked through the scene with Detective Rhino. He had the chance to duck out the back door and never see this incident, but he didn't.

Instead, they continued to walk down the narrow hallway to the living room. Detective White's mind burned with the photographs that covered the left wall. The frames hung over the brown paneled wall. The little girl he had just documented smiled as she stood for a school photo, her beautiful smile shining in the image. The picture below it showed another young girl about ten years old, as happy as could be.

The minute he turned the corner, the little ray of sunshine emerging from the photographs disintegrated into nothing but clouds of ash.

The hallway had opened up to the living room where a sofa was against the right wall and seated on the right side of the sofa was the mother with no apparent injury visible. Her eyes were hollow, and her gaze was empty as she stared straight ahead, unblinking. To her right was seated the young girl from the photographs, we suspected it was her at the least.

When he saw the girl, he could feel his legs give up and all the energy be punched out of him by an invisible force. The mother had a 357 revolver in her hand, which she had clearly used to shoot the young girl in the face, a face no longer present. The mother had then pointed the gun to her own chest and pulled the trigger.

Detective White stood his ground and gathered what strength he had in him, then slowly turned to meet Detective Rhino's similar gaze.

"I'm sorry, but I have to do this", he said walking over to the body. He gently lifted the jaw to reassemble the face partly.

Detective White nodded and walked over to him, trying to get a decent enough picture to confirm she was, in fact, the girl in the photos on the hallway wall.

They continued to process the gruesome scene but were distracted by a strange scratching noise. They were alone in the trailer, and each time they heard the noise they looked at each other as if to ask, "Can you tell what it is?" "Rats!" exclaimed Rhino as they returned back to work, measuring and photographing the bodies and surroundings. White was taking a final overall photo when the noise was heard in the area of the sofa. This time the silence was broken by White's girlish outburst "shit!" when a small grey & white face peered through the cushions next to the mother's body, then quickly disappeared again.

Detective White sat in the car alone with nothing but the haunting victim images in his mind. He took a deep breath and looked up towards the empty street. The ambulance had gone with the bodies, and the remaining officers were finishing up as a terrified rookie officer rushed out of the trailer motioning for the detectives to return.

Detective Rhino walked out and locked eyes with Detective White. The two nodded. Detective

White started his car then drove off. The horror of his work had caught up to him, and as they dug deeper, he found more shreds of evidence that confirmed the similarities of the victims to his daughters. The older child was close to his daughter in age, and the first name was the same.

What was truly chilling was how the younger daughter's birthday was only days apart from his youngest daughter's birthday, with similar characteristics evident in the photos.

Both Rhino and White had taken frequent breaks in the documentation of this scene, but they finally were able to push through the task. The incident and images were seldom mentioned after that day except for one minor detail. It was simply too much to bear, even for cops.

The one thing they were able to talk about openly was the fear that was instilled in the young rookie's eyes who came running out of the trailer when they were done because the scratching noise had greeted him. Despite the horror of the crime scene, it appears that a kitten was hidden in the sofa, only to emerge when the chaos had subsided and scared the rookie officer to death.

CHAPTER 7

A PERFECT MURDER

Marion Johnson was a woman who had lived her life on the darker side. However, when she met her husband, Gavin, she was convinced her life would take a turn for the best. He was everything she needed in a man, and he made her happy. After she married Gavin, he was finally able to be himself and show her his true colors.

Marion Johnson began to put up with the abuse she was so used to once again. In the darkness that consumed her life, a little ray of sunshine managed to crawl its way through. Marion was blessed with a daughter who Gavin had named Alyssa and treated her well. Being his daughter, Alyssa was safe from her mother's fate.

When September 5, 2003, came around, Marion had woken up like every other day. She was no longer surprised by the abuse that came her way with each passing day. This time something was different. Gavin had told her that he had a surprise planned for her the next day.

Instead of being excited, she feared what it might be. Marion knew better than anyone that Gavin's surprises often meant more torment for her. What truly put her off was the timing; her birthday was only a few days ago, and Gavin would always be riled up for at least a week after. She knew better than to come in front of him that day.

Marion's eyes opened at the blaring of the alarm that ripped the silence. She lay there lazily, then reached out and shut the alarm. She groaned. Somehow, even the rising sun streaming into the little room didn't make her feel better.

She welcomed the silence, but her ears strained at the sound of something clanking around in the next room. Slowly, she pushed herself off the bed. After getting ready for the day, she went to explore the computer room where Gavin had been sleeping the past few months. Before she could reach it, Gavin closed the door.

Marion stood there for a while, sighed, and then walked past it to the living room. Alyssa was seated on the sofa, waiting for her breakfast. Her eyes were glued to the little figures dancing and singing on the television screen. Marion walked into the kitchen and prepared a bowl of cereal, her mind buzzing with thoughts.

"Alyssa, come get your cereal", she called and immediately saw the little girl hopping to the table. Marion turned towards the sink when she heard a door open, and Gavin's familiar threatening aura greeted her before he did. His footsteps were erratic, and he seemed to create a fuss over nothing trying to pick a fight.

He was shouting at Marion, who tried to ignore him. The next thing she knew, a cereal bowl went whizzing past her head and smashed on the wall behind her. Shards of glass fell all over the floor and Alyssa's screams rang through the room. Marion's heart raced, and all she could think of then was her scared little girl caught amid a violent episode. Panicked, she grabbed Alyssa and retreated into the computer room where the house phone was located.

"You're not taking Alyssa anywhere!" Gavin's voice made its way to her, drowning the sound of

his heavy footsteps as he ran towards her. Alyssa fussed and cried in her arms, terrified. Marion picked up the phone and dialed 911, right when Gavin came bursting through the door as she dropped the phone.

"Alyssa, go and watch cartoons," Gavin screamed at her while she ran out of the room. Marion stood there, frozen and terrified. Only when Alyssa left did she notice the dishcloth and a brown bottle in his hands. A look of menace had come over his face.

"Why do you have a bottle of Chloroform?" Marion asked, her voice shaking.

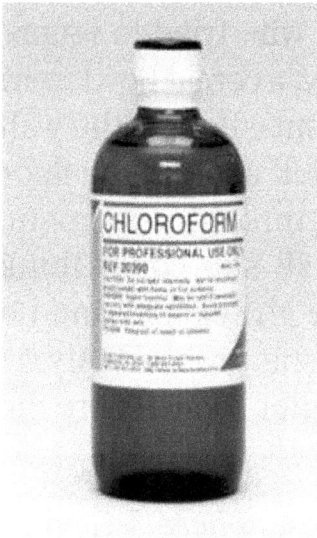

"I swear to god, you're going to be out just like that," Gavin replied calmly.

"Then you're going to wake up in the fucking lake," he added. He was now making his way to her as Marion backed up, tears filling her eyes.

"Don't do this to me," she begged, her voice trembling.

"Where did you get the bottle? People are going to know about this," she said.

"You left me. You went to Junction City, and never came back," he said.

"I called the cops," said Marion.

Gavin saw the receiver on the floor and picked it up. He threw the phone against the wall in an attempt to destroy it. *"No, no, please,"* Marion begged. Tears had begun to stream down her face.

"It'll be over in a second. You won't feel a thing," he said as he inched closer.

In a desperate attempt to protect herself Marion began to throw things at him, trying to keep him away. She reached for a stick with a sharp end and tried to keep him at bay for what seemed to be hours. No help had arrived yet, and she didn't know if it would. What was taking the police so long?

✪   ✪   ✪

When the call arrived, the dispatchers receiving the call were at first left confused. They tried to listen but were unable to get any details of what was happening. They couldn't determine where the call came from to render aid.

Every now and then, they heard Marion's terrified voice begging for a chance. Knowing that there was still time, the dispatcher called a few more people, and together they were able to figure out from the names they heard, "Marion & Gavin" to be the address on Maple for Gavin Johnson. The dispatcher remembered the address from a previous case.

Officers were immediately dispatched to intervene. Within a few minutes of figuring out the address, cops arrived at the address in Ogden, KS, only to realize that the right address was Maple Lane in Manhattan, almost 20 miles away.

The officers were holding the hope that Marion was still alive as officers from Manhattan were dispatched to a closer location. Marion felt that hours had passed since she made the call. The Johnson residence finally came into view and the team of police cars sped towards it. They rushed towards the door hearing the screams of a little girl as soon as they reached the yard.

When cops broke down the door, they immediately saw Gavin standing over his wife and Marion holding a stick in her hand as she tried to keep him at bay. At the sight of them, Marion's knees buckled, and she wept out of relief. The police took control of Gavin, putting him in handcuffs and escorting him out of the house. Marion grabbed Alyssa, holding her tight.

Officer Boyd walked into the scene then, looking around the house and walking up to Marion.

"Hello, I'm Officer Boyd. I was hoping we could interview you," he said to a visibly shaken Marion.

Marion's eyes still stuck to the door.

"What's going to happen to him?" Marion asked.

"He will be charged with Aggravated Assault. Don't worry. You and your child are safe now," Officer Boyd answered reassuringly.

Marion and Alyssa were escorted to the police station for an interview. If there was ever a poster child for battered wife syndrome, Marion was it. Officer Boyd helped her sit in one of the interview rooms and handed her a bottle of water as he took out a notepad. Fresh tears rolled down Marion's face as she held onto Alyssa, afraid of letting her go.

Officer Boyd, a seasoned officer with 18 years on patrol, began her interview trying to decipher Marion's story as she cried recalling the events leading up to the 911 call.

"He was trying to kill me. He told me that... he said he was... going to knock me out with the chloroform and kill me. I have been in an abusive relationship for years and lived each day in fear, not knowing when he would hurt me. A part of me knew he never would come to this extent, yet here we..." she began to sob again.

Officer Boyd nodded sympathetically as he took Marion's hand.

"He's gone now. He'll never hurt you again," he said. Marion pulled back clearly frightened by his contact. Marion again was withdrawn, and inconsolable with fear, so the interview was terminated for now.

After the medics cleared Alyssa and Marion of injuries, the police made their way back to the trailer with them, returning them home, leaving the little home to its haunting memories. Officer Boyd's mind raced back and forth to the interview. His heart wasn't quite settled on the story, and he knew something was there that he needed to check up on.

Officer Boyd walked into the investigation division and asked for help from the Detective on duty, Detective Carla Black. He explained how the call had come in and the delay in the response. He then explained the story Marion had provided and how she was severely withdrawn, a classic case of battered wife syndrome. Officer Boyd left her stating that there was clearly more to the story, but it was going to take a patient detective to sift through the tears to get to the truth.

Det. Black walked into the new set of offices where Detective Brad White sat. He peered up through his glasses as he heard the click of her heels approaching him.

"Hey, Brad, I need your help. I need a search warrant for the Johnson residence, and I need you to look into the 911 call recording for me," she said and handed him a file.

"I also need a CVSA". (Computerized Voice Stress Analysis) White responded that he would get started on the search warrants, but he needed to get Officer Tiller in internal affairs to do the CVSA to maximize their efforts.

When she informed him about the mix-up in houses, Detective White immediately agreed to it. There was something about the case that intrigued him. He didn't know that the deeper he investigated, the more he would learn things were hidden under the surface of this case.

When Detective White heard the recording, he couldn't figure anything out either. All he heard were distant screams, and it was enough to keep him searching for more. His extensive training and development helped him in gaining insight into this case as well.

It was only a few years back that Detective White had promised himself that he would take his skills in computer programming to the next level. Fate had favored him then, and he then ended up befriending fellow Hi-Tech investigators in Wichita, KS.

These were the people who had been working on a 30-year-old Cold Case involving a suspect they had just discovered "Dennis Raider" The BTK Killer (Bind, Torture, Kill). Raider was identified after he used a computer in the local church to create a floppy disc. He had left that disk for the investigators, taunting them that they had been unable to find him in the past 30 years.

Unknown to Raider, the disc contained META Data, which embeds bits of information about the computer used to create the disc. It was this information that led the investigators to Raider and his subsequent arrest.

Working on Marion's recording was nothing new for Detective White. As soon as he heard it, he knew precisely what he had to do. Detective White first isolated the voices and then proceeded by removing the background noises. Soon enough, it was evident what was happening on the other side of the call. He noted it all down.

"Marion - Why are you getting a bottle of chloroform?

Gavin - I swear to god you're going to be out just like that.

Gavin - Then you're going to wake up in the fucking lake

Marion - Don't do this to me

Marion - Where did you get the bottle?

Marion - People are going to know about this

Gavin - You left me, you went to Junction City, and never came back.

Marion - I called the cops."

While many of their exchanges went unheard, this was more than enough information to visualize what had happened. As the day came to an end, Brad White knew there was plenty more work to be done.

Once the recordings were heavily investigated, Detective White began his thorough research into the personal computers. He knew the incident at Marion's house was premeditated from her tear-filled explanation. He then went through Gavin's computer but found that it had been wiped clean with a program called CyberScrub, which was scheduled to run daily. This was not a coincidence to learn Gavin was covering his tracks, but Gavin didn't know that nothing is really deleted on your computer hard drive.

For Detective White, it was easy enough to navigate through the layers of a criminal cover-up after the file index was repaired/reconstructed. He spent hours in the bustle of the station, sitting in front of his computer. Finally, he found the reference to chloroform and a 96- page document from ScienceLab.com.

Jackpot, he thought, smiling to himself. He read through the document, which explained all the uses for the solvent, and more importantly, the effects of exposure.

Detective White scanned through it, reading the details of the ratio of chloroform required to render a person incapacitated from the exposure. However, this wasn't all he found. His digging identified a reference to a purchase of said chloroform LC2870-500ml on 08- 14-2003, which was mailed to the Maple address at a cost of only $46.21. It also clarified the paper trail.

However, there were other interesting things found which revealed this was in the plans longer than the police initially thought:

- 08-14-2003 – Det. White found more research at ATSDR-TOXFAQS for chloroform,
- 08-02-2003 – Chloroform interaction research at Drug Digest
- 07-28-2003 – How to change your identity
- 07-28-2003 – How to get lost and stay that way
- 05-01-2003 – Anonymous Internet Surfing
- 05-01-2003 – FarOut Anonymous Remailer

"How to Change Your Identity"

How to Get Lost — And Stay That Way!

Plus Your Second Bonus Report: The Perfect Resume

It took Detective White a few days but eventually, he had enough information for Detective Black. He walked to her cubicle a week after she had approached him about the case with his hands full of files.

"I've got all the evidence for the Johnson case,"

White said.

"Looks like someone's been working hard!" she said, a pleased expression on her face as she looked at the files.

"Just doing my job," Detective White said, smiling.

When he left, Detective Black began sifting through the files. Once she was confident, she had enough information, she knew it was time to pay Marion a visit once again.

✪   ✪   ✪

The sun had risen well overhead, and the heat was palpating through the city. Detective Black pulled up at the house with Detective White. She knew that if anyone could talk about the evidence, it would be Detective White. She braced herself for the heat as she opened the door and stepped out.

The house seemed calm as she walked through the dead yard and knocked on the door.

"Who is it?"

"Detective Carla Black from RCPD," Detective Black replied as she saw the curtain from the side window move. A minute later, the door opened.

"Hello, detective, please come in," Marion said, appearing much more relaxed than when she was interviewed at the police department. Detective Black walked inside the dim living room and sat on the sofa. Alyssa was close by watching television.

"I just wanted to check up on how you were doing and if you could provide me with more information from the incident. This is my partner, Detective Brad White," Detective Black began.

Once the introductions were done, Detective Black started to pursue questions about the incident. She realized she had to push Marion for information, even though it had occurred a few days ago. Regardless of how much Detective Black pushed her, she only provided bits of information at a time.

"The trauma is more significant than we realized," Detective White whispered as Marion

stood up to get them a glass of water. He looked around the room. A second television was broken, and there were patches of paint peeling from the walls. Once she returned, Detective White sat up and began to talk to her about the evidence found on the computer.

"As per our investigations, it's evident that Gavin had been planning this for several months. Is there anything he could have said to you about it before this?" Detective White asked.

Marion looked down and began to think. Suddenly, her eyes widened as she recalled an incident.

"Well, he did say during a fight that he intended to throw me off the Turtle Creek Dam while I was unconscious. He said it was so I would drown in the lake. He told me he had been telling friends for months that I was suicidal and that no one would question him when they found my body," Marion said, her voice trembling once again.

It was all that they needed to charge Gavin Johnson.

While they wanted to continue the interview, it was nearly impossible, given that Marion had become inconsolable once again.

They walked out of the house, satisfied. However, something bugged Detective White. He knew it couldn't be so easy, so he sought an expert witness about the chloroform. However, for that to happen, he needed to know who to approach. Finding someone was his next challenge.

As the day turned to dusk and he made his way home, he passed by a local hospital and immediately knew it was the place to go. There was no questioning that medical professionals all knew each other and their specialties.

An anesthesiologist is the way to go. He said to himself as he turned the car to the parking lot and walked into the hospital. He tried to think past the intense smell of medicines that welcomed him.

After a few questions, he was directed to Dr. Pelican, the most sought-after anesthesiologist specialist in town. Dr. Pelican was a silver-haired, well- distinguished man who was the type of person who immediately demanded attention by simply walking into the room.

Detective White was directed to his office and as he waited there, he saw the frame on his desk of the anesthesiologist holding an award. Finally, after a few moments of waiting, Dr. Pelican walked inside.

"Ah, Detective, I was informed you would be here," the doctor said and grabbed a seat. *"What can I help you with?"*

Detective White began his questioning, asking Dr. Pelican about the possibility of a suspect trying to use chloroform to knock his victim unconscious and then throw the victim into the lake as a means of covering up the cause of death. The mention of it made the doctor's eyebrows shoot up. He leaned forward with his hand under his chin.

"Well, that kind of murder does mean the killer might have put a great deal of thought into the plan. It was a great way to mask a murder as a suicide even if he didn't realize how clever his plan really was," the doctor said almost to himself. He then looked up at Detective White.

"You see, the chloroform would have clearly left the victim unable to defend themselves. And the victim wouldn't have woken up when they hit the water." He paused, then continued.

"However, that's something he could easily pick up from television. What's clever is that chloroform is water-soluble, which means that

the evidence of the chloroform would have been dissolved if this were a wet drowning."

"I'm sorry, wet drowning?" Detective White asked.

"Ah, yes. I see your confusion, and that is what makes this clever. There is only a small chance it wouldn't be a wet drowning destroying the evidence of the chloroform in the victim's system."

"Go on."

"A wet drowning is when the victim ingests water into the lungs and then drowns in the water. There is a lesser chance of a dry drowning, which is where the body anticipates the ingestion of the water, and the esophagus closes off, and the victim suffocates to death. This would have left evidence of the chloroform in the victim's system to be found in an autopsy." Dr. Pelican clarified.

It left Detective White even more baffled. This case had suddenly drawn much further interest than it was before.

"Interesting case you have, detective. Let me know how it ends up," Dr. Pelican said.

"Interesting, indeed. Well, thank you for your time," Detective White said and stood up,

shaking the doctor's hand. Dr. Pelican's words stuck to him.

Soon Gavin's case made it to court. It just so happened that even while facing the mounting evidence, he still protested his innocence. He opposed the results of the CVSA, which suggested that he was, in fact, trying to kill his wife, and went to the extent of submitting a polygraph examination for the attempted murder. As much as it was expected that he would be shown as a liar, the results came back as inconclusive.

The evidence all pointed to Gavin trying to kill her. That and the fact that Marion showed up almost every day at the station to relay bits of information about her abuse. She pleaded on each visit to keep him in jail. In the end, he could not generate bail, which was set at $250,000.00. Marion was relatively safe from her abuser.

But the tales she was telling were becoming more interesting and bizarre.

✪ ✪ ✪

CHAPTER 8

LIVING WITH A MANIAC

O ver the next few weeks, since the incident occurred, Marion frequented the station regularly with additional stories of abuse from Gavin. Sometimes, she seemed to be composed and other times she seemed overwhelmed by the memories surfacing in her mind. It was evident that Gavin was the bad guy. Every visit from Marion would make it more transparent.

She would come in looking like a strung-out meth addict even though it wasn't meth unraveling her but the reality of her life. Every time she came in, she would request for Detectives Black or White. If anyone else approached her, she would deny speaking to them and leave the station. She was only comfortable speaking to the detectives.

Most of the time, Detective Black was the only one sitting with her. Marion began her story from the beginning each time. Like every love-struck woman begins her journey, Marion described how she had met the man who had immediately stolen her heart.

It was a cold December night in Junction City, and Marion had made her way to a local bar to play darts and pool. The music played in the background as she looked around the room with a glass of beer in her hand. There in the distance, her eyes fell on a dark-haired man. Immediately, she was smitten.

It was evident that he too noticed her, as only a few moments later, he pulled away from the pool table and made his way to her. He was quite the master of words and knew exactly what to say to make Marion fall for him. That was all it took to make her his. Even as Marion spoke about him, there was a twinkle in her eyes from the memories.

"We spent so much time together. I just wish I had taken that time to know a little bit about him and his past," Marion had told Detective White. The lack of information that they got about Gavin's history meant that the detectives

had to do a little research independently. It was a challenge they were up for.

Detective White submitted an inquiry to the military for the records of Gavin Johnson. From the stories they learned from Marion and their thoughts about him were very different from what the research showed.

The research didn't all happen as quickly as they had hoped; simply getting a response from the military took three months. Although what they learned seemed to affect their research in a vastly different way.

It seemed that Gavin was not a very good soldier. He had entered the Army from a little town in Dumas, Arkansas, as one of two brothers. Both the brothers had very little to contribute to society. They were both offered an opportunity to join the military or go to jail for the multiple petty crimes they committed in their small quiet town.

It was evident from their options that the townsfolk wanted nothing to do with them. Instead of mandating them to serve time in jail and return to society to cause more trouble, they thought it was best to try to get them to enlist in the military and possibly put them on a better path.

Gavin's brother, George, took the opportunity to excel in the military. He never returned to Arkansas. It became evident that Gavin was the root of his troubles, so he cut all ties with him.

Unlike his brother, Gavin was stationed in the military as a cook at Ft. Hood, TX. He fought the system every step of the way and eventually ended up getting into trouble. It was difficult for him to break the habit of who he was. He eventually went back to the pattern of starting fights in basic training. Oddly even his terrible attitude didn't prevent him from graduating.

His first assignment was at FT. Hood. Again, destined to be himself, he got into trouble with things constantly disappearing from his unit. He would always act aloof and pretend as though he was no big deal.

What he did not realize was that he wasn't dealing with common people but the military. They discovered Gavin was selling military property and also stealing food.

Even through all the trouble, Gavin was smart. He knew how to work the system. He managed to keep his nose clean long enough to make it to the grade of Specialist E4. It didn't last long, though. Military life was tough, but not tough enough to change Gavin. He was set in his ways and knew what he had to and didn't have to do. He steered his life the way he wanted.

Eventually, Gavin laid his eyes on a woman he knew he needed to make his. Carol Schmitz was a young girl who had caught Gavin's attention, and she was a true beauty. He married Carol in 1986, but the marriage, much like every other relationship in his life, didn't last long. When he was reassigned to Fort Riley, Kansas, the couple lived in Junction City. Carol had realized then that there was darkness within Gavin, and it wasn't something he tried to cover.

Gavin wasn't interested in hiding who he was in front of Carol, and the couple would engage in prolonged heated arguments. It had gotten to the point that the police were often called to resolve domestic disputes. The main issue was Gavin's uncontrollable anger. His fits and outbursts came too frequently, and Carol saw the side of him that she began to despise. There was evil lurking behind Gavin's face. She had witnessed it way too much.

It wasn't long after they had gotten married that Carol decided she'd had enough of the constant arguments. Gavin was never the man to control his temper, and Carol wasn't ready to handle that. One day after another one of his outbursts, she screamed at him, telling him she needed a divorce.

What Carol didn't expect was the slap that reverberated across her skin. The stinging sensation that the imprint of his fingers left on her face burned as though she was branded. It was the last straw, and she would not stick around with a man who would go to such an extent. A few months into his marriage, Gavin found himself divorced and alone in Junction City.

On his own now, Gavin would wreak havoc wherever he went. He did, however, meet a girl who lived off-post. She had a baby, and during the time they were dating, tragedy struck the house and the baby died.

The military now had their eyes on Gavin, and caution was necessary. They decided that it was time he moved to the military housing with the rest of his unit. At the barracks, he avoided the police in any investigation they might be doing, and ultimately the death of the baby was ruled an accident.

Gavin was set in his ways and utterly unfazed by the incidents that unfolded around him. He held the darkness tight within him to keep him from feeling bad about anything that went wrong because of him. The unit noticed it, and their troubles with him only continued.

Gavin wasn't ready to change, no matter how much bad luck surrounded him. There was no other solution but to downgrade his rank with an Article 15 (Military discipline), reducing Gavin basically to a dishwasher in his unit. No one realized that this assignment made it relatively easy for him to fly under the radar. He spent his free time hustling the locals in the bars at the pool table or selling some half-baked scheme to make money. Even so, his record showed that he was set in the pattern he always had. He was constantly in trouble with the law. His record went as follows:

- October 1988 – he was arrested for shoplifting
- December 1988 – he was discharged from the Army

- 1989 – he filed for bankruptcy
- April 1992 – he was arrested for nine counts of worthless checks
- 1993 – he again filed for bankruptcy
- March of 1993 – he was arrested on Fort Riley for a DUI. The Military blotter report explained that Gavin had attempted to flee and elude the officers with a suspended license. The blotter listed his offenses as DUI, driving while suspended, fleeing and eluding, criminal trespassing, an exhibition of speed, battery on a law enforcement officer, and unlawful use of a weapon when he was holding the Military Police at bay with a pipe.

Gavin was the definition of a bad guy, with trouble arising wherever he went. Somehow it did not affect him. It wasn't long after this his courtship with Marion began.

As a whole, Gavin was able to keep it together as the up the good guy for Marion. He knew he needed to make it work with Marion. He was determined to convince her that he was the man she had been searching for. To everyone who knew Gavin, it seemed as though Marion opened a side of him that no one had seen.

All of a sudden, Gavin was a better person. Marion was happy, and he did everything in his power to keep her happy. On September 21, 1995, Marion stood at the altar in a white dress, holding Gavin's hands and reciting her vows.

A couple of years later, in 1997, Gavin left his job at an ICE manufacturing company. Both he and Marion joined KFC together and purchased a Red 1991 Pontiac Sunbird, which was registered in Marion's parent's name. Contrary to what the public saw, their lives began to teeter downward fast.

That year, Gavin was investigated for trying to start an escort business. However, the lack of prostitutes working for him meant that the case was never developed into an arrestable offense. Once again, Gavin went under the radar until the year came closer to an end.

While a suspect in a case Gavin purchased a Ruger P95 9mm from a gun shop in Ogden, KS. It was reported he was following a female employee home and wouldn't leave. Since there was no arrest or conviction, he was able to purchase the handgun.

The happy family that everyone saw was now riddled with secrets. The problems were only beginning to get worse, especially for Marion. Marion was still hopeful that the New Year would deliver new possibilities. Marion and Gavin spent 1998 trying to settle down and rebuild their lives. Soon the happiness flourished as they made their way towards 1999.

Suddenly things began to change in the house. Gavin started talking to Marion about having a gun in the house even though he had purchased it a year ago without telling her. This was information that didn't settle well with Marion. She was afraid of accidents happening and having a gun in the house only made her more scared. Instead, she insisted that he keep the gun in the shed outside.

Gavin was never the type to pay heed to her words or anyone else's advice. For that reason, he persisted in his attempts to make Marion understand how to handle the gun. Marion, on the other hand, was much too afraid of it. Unknowingly, Marion had shown Gavin her weakness, and he took it.

Knowing how much Marion feared having a gun in the house gave Gavin a sense of control and he kept it with him. He threatened to use it even more than before. Once, during an argument over the gun, Gavin pulled it out and pointed it at her head. She stood still, frozen, as tears pooled in her eyes. She saw the wickedness glimmering in his eyes as he pulled the trigger.

She heard the "CLICK" from the empty chamber and finally breathed again. She fell on her knees, sobbing as he smiled at his successful attempt to scare her. Now he kept the gun away in the shed.

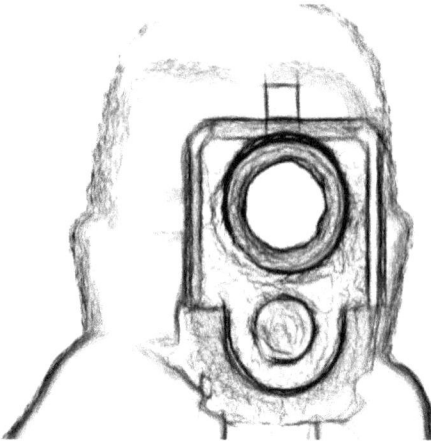

Year 1999 was contemptuous, but it was also the year Marion received the happiness of new life growing inside her body. Just two weeks after the pregnancy was realized by Gavin, the police were called once again for a domestic complaint.

Gavin began to have many undesirable events. He quit his job at a plumbing company only three weeks after the police were called to his home. As Marion awaited his return home, Gavin was arrested for a DUI, this time driving the Red Pontiac.

Just when Marion thought things would work out well with her marriage, Gavin's true colors showed. The darkest side of him was revealed, and she had to face the consequences of the man she had chosen. It was the summer of 1999 when Gavin developed a friendship with a coworker, Dana, at KFC. However, it didn't just remain a friendship; Gavin was infatuated by Dana to the point that he stalked her, as he had done to the girl before Marion.

Dana was not familiar with Gavin and his capabilities or his temper. One night as she was on a date with her boyfriend in a local park, Gavin waited for her boyfriend to leave to make his approach as Dana was walking to her apartment only yards away. Once the boyfriend was out of sight, Gavin forced her to go to her apartment, where he raped her.

Traumatized, Dana could not work there anymore, where she would have to see her rapist every day. Still, she was so filled with fear that she never reported the rape until directly questioned about her relationship with Gavin. During an interview in 2003, she explained that there had been other employees who fell victim to him that summer in 1999, but she could not provide details of what specifically happened to them. She only knew Gavin had pursued them as well and feared what had occurred to her would happen to them.

Gavin's relationship with Marion only worsened. They had yet another domestic fight where the police were called. This time, however, he was arrested, but it was on a completely different charge. Gavin was arrested for the possession of marijuana. He ended up serving five days in jail.

Marion was blessed with her baby girl amongst the darkness in October of 1999, and Marion quit her job to pay more attention to her newborn daughter, Alyssa.

Coincidentally, during that same time, Gavin quit KFC as well and started working for Schwan's until he had a complaint filed against him that he had been caught entering someone's home in nearby Leonardville. His next job with a sheet metal business had Gavin driving through Leonardville every day. This made it easy for Gavin to continue his malicious schemes until the tragic day, December 15, 1999.

Marion began to stutter at this point, finding it difficult to continue with her recollections.

"It's very difficult to recall the events over the years after Alyssa's birth and how our money issues escalated," Marion told Detective White. However, she still tried to continue the best she could.

For the next two years through 2001, Gavin continued to bounce around with jobs until April 2002 when many things changed. Gavin went back to his habit of writing bad checks with a risky increase. He took out two loans for $3962.99 and $6000.00. Gavin tried to explain how the money was spent to Marion, but she didn't understand it.

In June 2002, Gavin then created a fake check on Landmark Bank for $29,873.21, which he made payable to himself from a fraudulent business, Knoxberry Co. Needless to say, it didn't work, and his bank charged him for the amount. Of course, Gavin wasn't all too happy about it. Subpoenas were issued for him to appear in court to be held accountable for the bad check.

This wasn't enough for Gavin, and before he was expected in court, Gavin created another check written in October 2002 for $25,000.00 from Birch Telecom, a legitimate company. He continued and made two more for $5,200.00 and $3,500.00 from Micron PC, also a legitimate company, but all of the checks were fake with no funds to back them up.

Finally, in January of 2003, all the checks caught up with him when he was arrested for forgery and theft. He was never too happy about being caught, and as always, Marion had to face the worst of it.

Two months later, March 31, 2003, Marion had gone out with a few of her friends to get away from Gavin. Even then, she trusted Gavin with Alyssa, his daughter, and was comfortable with leaving her in his care. When she returned home after a much-needed respite, she found the house dark. An ominous feeling filled her, and as she entered the living room.

Marion found Gavin on the floor with beer cans all around him. He was very drunk, and she knew better than to come close to him. She tried her best to tiptoe past him when her foot hit an empty beer can on the floor, creating a ruckus that woke him up.

The drunken Gavin woke up and began his persistent yelling, threatening to kill her someday with no one ever suspecting him as the one to do it. Marion was in tears as she related the incident, and the fear was evident in her eyes. Gavin told her his plan to throw her in the lake with his nasty demeanor. He made it known to her that he was capable of doing something very extreme.

Marion related her memory of how she tried to get him to go to bed and stop the argument. Gavin grew so insistent in his attempts to scare her he then opened up the computer and showed her a photo of an older woman on the KBI (Kansas Bureau of Investigations) website. Marion trembled as she told the detectives she was aware of the reward for information on the murder of Olive Stumpp.

Marion was terrified of Gavin, but never thought he would be capable of doing something like this. She immediately dismissed him and his story, but he continued to explain that it was him. She told how he kept telling her that he had killed the woman in the photo.

Gavin told Marion he could prove it as he walked her through how he previously parked his car near the golf course and walked to her house in the snow. He told her that he had shot her in the basement of the house twice to make sure she was dead. He also described what she was wearing when he killed her. He gave her information that only people who were there would know. Gavin told Marion that Olive Stumpp was wearing a Christmas sweater when he killed her. This information was not made public.

Marion tried to talk to him the following day about the news Gavin shared about murdering Olive Stumpp. This sparked an argument with Gavin, who said it was just an earlier April fool's joke. His eyes were intense when he said he never wanted her to mention Olive Stumpp again.

In June of 2003, things started to fall apart as the preliminary hearing for the forgery cases proceeded. Gavin heard the testimony from Detective Stevens about all the counterfeit checks. The bank staff also pushed for the prosecution, including Ms. Jo.

The effort to discredit Det. Steven's case went on, and that was when Ms. Jo received an email allegedly from Det. Stevens. This email was loaded with sexual overtones and suggested that the two of them had a steamy affair. When Ms. Jo received a second email on August 29, 2003, she knew that it was time to contact the police.

The captain of the investigation started an internal affairs investigation, not knowing if any of the allegations were true. However, shortly after the 911 call on September 6, 2003, the Captain approached Det. White to look into how these emails might have been sent.

Detective White had already been approached about the search warrant for the computer at the Johnson residence, so he took a second look at the contents of the computer and found the information needed to clear Det. Stevens.

Det. White found that Gavin had used a VPN (Virtual Private Network) to create a masked email, making it look like Det. Stevens had sent it from the police department email server. With this information Det. White scheduled an interview with Gavin, who was already in the Riley County jail.

During the interview, Gavin seemed proud as he acknowledged that he had, in fact, sent the emails in an effort to discredit Det. Stevens. Moreover, he was impressed that Det. White was able to unravel his methods. He called Det. White "MacGyver" and continued to do so from this point forward into the homicide investigation when things took a very different turn.

CHAPTER 9

FACT OR FICTION

Marion's continued visits to the station had become so repetitive in verse that Detective Black became annoyed by her. Marion repeated the same things over and over again. Det. Black would cringe every time she received a call that Marion Johnson was waiting in the lobby.

Jokingly she would look for Det. White, and say it was his turn. While she did receive some new information with every visit it was sometimes hard to sift through the strange, completely irrelevant, or old information Marion was providing to get a single slice of something that would be useful.

Marion's stories were certainly bizarre over the last few months and seemingly correct. What the officers didn't know was if Gavin had researched the information and shared it with Marion to scare her or if he really participated in acting them out. They could not be sure.

Both Detective Black and Detective White spent most days trying to decipher Marion's information to determine credibility. Detective Black's ledgers were now filled with questions, "Did Gavin have a gun? Did Gavin have a motive? Did Gavin have an opportunity?"

Keeping all these questions in mind, they dug through many news articles. Nothing was going in Gavin's favor. When they talked about the case that Detectives Fleck and Detective Ryan had worked on together, they learned the men had prepared an arrest warrant for John Fuller as the murderer of Olive Stumpp. It was waiting to be signed by a judge and served.

It had been years since the murder, and their lead added a new turn to the case. The detectives were convinced that John Fuller was guilty of murdering Olive Stumpp and Gavin was just a henchman pumping his ego to his wife.

Soon the county prosecutor was listening to the evidence and considered signing the arrest warrant. He insisted that Detective White and

Detective Black work on the case full-time and thus determine if the lead was actually true or whether they continue with the prosecution of John Fuller as the killer of Olive Stumpp.

The new lead ended up creating tension within the investigation department dividing the old and new investigation teams and pitting them against one another for truth. Which of the evidence trails was false?

The tension grew to solve the case. Interestingly, Gavin was the only person who shared his stories with Marion about Olive wearing a Christmas sweater over her clothes. This detail was never released anywhere. He had told Marion about it when drunk and trying to convince her about his evil deed.

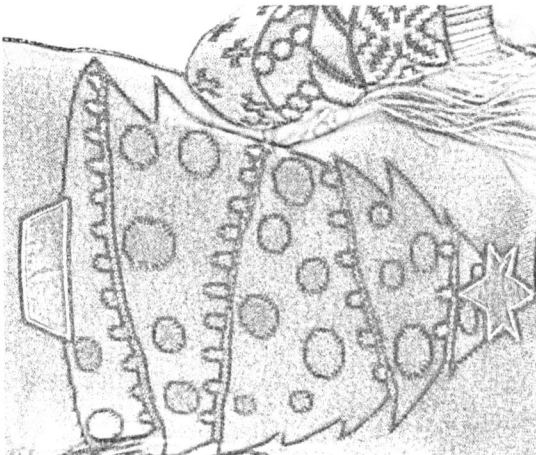

The lead role for the investigation was handed over to Detectives Black and White to determine the validity of Gavin as the murderer. They scattered the briefing room with paper creating a timeline of events. They began with the date of the homicide and the whereabouts of Gavin who was in town or the vicinity at the time of the crime.

Gavin had been working at Clay Center and commuting through Leonardville every morning. He also had a pawn shop receipt showing that he had a Rugger P95, the same model of the gun which took Olive's life. The two detectives reluctantly turned their attention back to questioning Marion, this time trying to focus her on the Stumpp murder details.

They learned from Marion, Gavin, and her son, Kevin, took a trip to Arkansas to install a satellite TV for Gavin's parents shortly after the murder. The trip was confirmed through subscription activation with Direct TV. There was no real connection that could be built between the two to determine a motive.

The detectives began to issue subpoenas to assist in the investigation. They sent inquisitions to all the banks, the military, and an extensive background check to learn more about how Gavin could have gotten away with this for so long and originally missed as a suspect or person of interest in the initial case.

Looking back at the pawnshop records, the detectives discovered Gavin had pawned his Ruger P95 on November 19th, 1999, for $200, then retrieved it on December 7th, 1999, just in time for the murder. That provided him with means.

When they looked at the Bank Records, they saw that he had actually visited the Leonardville Bank on November 19th, 1999. At the bank, he opened an account by forging Marion's name. This was overlooked in the original investigation. Det. Lufkin only looked at the active accounts instead of all accounts. He had failed to see the account opened on the 19th and closed just four days later. More importantly he missed that the account was opened & closed with Olive Stumpp.

As the detectives looked deeper into the case, they discovered Olive had made a note on the card when the account was closed, with a question mark in the margin. John Fuller was not connected to the bank, and any arrest if made would be on speculation of his bad reputation. Fuller had no physical evidence which directly connected him to the crime, no boots, no gun, no direct witnesses, but plenty of friends & enemies telling stories in hopes of collecting the reward.

CIRCUMSTANTIAL EVIDENCE

Fuller was said to have disposed of the gun in his grandmother's yard. Det. White and others spent an entire day with ground-penetrating radar and shovels digging hundreds of holes, still no gun was found. Did Gavin have the right gun in his possession at the time of the murder?

Detectives had speculation from witnesses who suspected Fuller of this crime, but none that could provide any direct evidence. The detectives also now had a drunken confession from Gavin but was it enough because he had provided some details that were never released to the public. The only thing left to do now was to prove the murder happened by Gavin without having the gun or any physical evidence placing him at the scene.

As Detective White continued to look through the records, something caught his eye.

"The boot prints," he said.

Gavin did have small feet. Once they checked his shoes at his home, they found that they were all a size 8.5 rather than the 8 from the crime scene, and no hiking boots to match those from the crime. Detective White thought about it and decided it could still be used, not all shoe sizes are the same. By now, it seemed as though they were on the right trail. All that was left to do was connect the dots and ensure that each element of the crime fit into Gavin's timeline. That would allow them to make the arrest.

Detective White did as much research as he could while juggling another case he was working on. It was a homicide from Lawrence, Kansas, involving a college professor of linguistics at Kansas State University suspected of killing his wife, a former criminal prosecutor. It was said that the husband killed his wife over a child custody dispute.

The detectives involved in the other case from Douglas County had a little wager to see who would be able to get their arrest first. Detective White knew that there were no shortcuts when it came to a homicide investigation. All the elements had to be met to ensure a successful prosecution.

As far as Olive Stumpp's case was concerned, Detective White was excited about the headway he was making with Gavin. Finally, things seemed to be looking up.

As for the Professor's case, that's a story for another day.

CHAPTER 10

THE COLD CASE

PART 1

There was still a long way to go with Gavin. Detective White began spending his days behind seventeen, two-inch-thick binders from the original case. His mind was soaking in all the information, interviews, and tips, which may or may not be accurate now with the new leads from Marion. The more he learned about the case, the more he and Detective Black knew that they needed to do more background investigation on Gavin.

The best way forward was to walk in Gavin's shoes from the beginning so they could learn if any new subpoenas could shine a huge spotlight on motive. The more they looked, the more they learned about how Gavin managed his finances. With each financial setback he encountered, Gavin did something desperate to try to fix his situation.

AUGUST 5TH, 1965

It was a dark Saturday morning when Gavin was born. The sounds of his cries echoed through the hospital halls. Gavin's mother held him in her arms and caressed his face until he quieted down. Slowly he calmed down and went into a slumber as she handed him to the nurse.

"Take him away," she said, her voice cold. The nurse quickly took the boy out of the room, and his mother closed her eyes, allowing herself to sleep.

Gavin's parents loved him but couldn't keep away from the fact that he was a mistake and not planned. It wasn't until his brother entered his life that Gavin noticed the difference between the attention he got, and his brother received. He began to act out to gain attention. Gavin's father, who often came home drunk, would take a belt to Gavin while his mother watched, and his brother ran scot-free.

It made him angry, but he had control over it. Gavin became known around his neighborhood as the boy who hurt animals. Wherever he went, there was always a trail of dead or injured animals in his wake.

Once, he had taken a kitten home only to have his mother scream at him. Instead of leaving the kitten outside, Gavin took the kitten and bent its leg until he heard it break. Its painful shrieks erupted, and Gavin was punished with a time out, and by time out, I mean locked in his room while the kitten was disposed of on the street. Since money was tight, Gavin's mother knew she wouldn't be able to afford any punitive charges against Gavin for the incident, so she left the kitten in a dumpster close by.

Gavin only became angrier over time, and it was worse since he was the "odd child" in school. He wasn't just always picked on, but sometimes he would be the bully as well. Intimidated by the stuff that everyone around him had, he would find ways to get them as well. His mother would find money missing from her purse every now and then, and his dad would be ready with a belt.

Gavin began stealing at an early age. He always targeted the easy targets first including his parents and family. While he had to face the consequences when he was caught, it hardly ever affected him. Eventually, he dragged his brother into doing the same, offering assistance to him in the tricks he had learned over time.

However, when he couldn't find enough, and his need grew, Gavin knew there was more that he had to do. Slowly, his attention moved to breaking into cars and anything he could steal that would get him money from selling on the streets.

As time went on, both Gavin and his brother increased their petty theft to bigger, more expensive items they took. It was all about the bigger prize. How much could they take?

Gavin loved the attention. He wanted to be known and feared by those who knew him. This was a way to gain him notoriety on the streets.

One day he came home and found his brother going through his hidden stash of stolen goods in his bedroom.

"Where did you get these?" His brother asked as he picked up a diamond necklace from one of the boxes. His eyes widened at the glittering stones.

Gavin walked over to him and shoved him aside until he toppled over. He was raging to have his brother find his goods.

"What the fuck are you doing in my room?! I told you never to come in here," he screamed, but his brother wasn't going to be bullied by Gavin. He stood up and jumped over to Gavin as he readied his fist to punch him in the face. Gavin grabbed him and threw him against the wall, taking him in a chokehold.

"Whatever we steal, we do it together, and you know that," he seethed, making Gavin release him. They talked about it and Gavin agreed to have him come along.

"I want to go big," Gavin said, smiling.

What do you have in mind?" his brother asked, sitting down. The two plotted all night. After that, their alliance managed to bring them items they had never thought they would have. However, the bigger they went, the more difficult it became for them to hide the things. They had now managed to get things from electronics to cars to jewelry and everything in between.

However, their luck didn't last as long as he would have liked. Only a month after, the brothers were caught on a plan to break into a church. Gavin had planned to steal the band's equipment consisting of electric guitars and keyboards, drums, and amplifiers. Along with him and his brother, he had also recruited some older friends who had a car. They were going to get in and out with this equipment to start a band. It was going to be something along the lines of JADK, 'Just Another Dumbas Kid.'

This was the start of a major change that took place in Gavin's life. Being a juvenile (17), he wasn't too worried about the consequences that would befall them if they were caught. They did get caught and their judge was the man from their town, fittingly called DUMAS. He was running for re-election and needed a gesture that would make him look good in the public's eyes.

When Gavin's case came up, the judge saw his opportunity. Over the years, Gavin had often disrupted the town and ended up in jail, but this time would be different. His name was already known around town as a hoodlum, and the judge knew he had to do something that called attention to the repeat offender. After thinking about it, he found that his solution was to offer the juvenile delinquents an option to join the military on their 18th birthday instead of juvenile detention until their 21st birthday.

✪ ✪ ✪

Looking back, Brad could empathize with the judge's decisions. He had probably thought it was a good idea to rehabilitate juveniles. Gavin was not an ordinary juvenile. He had all the makings of a psycho-killer. The trauma he had faced at the hands of his father and the bullies had turned him into a monster.

The more Detective White put the pieces together about Gavin's past, the more the cases began to make sense. All the pieces of the puzzle in the Stumpp's murder case were fitting together.

THE CAR

When Marion and Gavin got married, their lives had begun great. They were like any other newlyweds, madly in love and always happy. Marion's family was happy with them, too. Their parents did not know any reason not to be happy for their marriage. The only problem was a vehicle. All they had was an old beat-up Ford Taurus that continually broke down and was undependable.

It wasn't much of a problem for Gavin; he was used to having issues at work and not showing up on time. Marion was always on time and a good employee spurring a fight about buying a new car. It was time for them to have a reliable car. With the money problems they had, there was no way they could afford a new car. There was only one thing left to do.

Marion swallowed her pride and asked her parents for help. At first, they were just going to give them a little money to help. Gavin wanted her parents to purchase the car for them. He talked to them and was able to convince them to fund the car completely as long as it was in their name.

It was then that the couple was able to purchase a 1991 Maroon Pontiac Sunbird. It was a good car and Marion loved driving it. Unfortunately, Gavin got a job in Clay Center so she was no longer the main person using the vehicle. He was now using the car to commute to work, and who knows what else.

As Detective White looked through the documents, he found that the route to Clay Center was through Leonardville. As Gavin made the trips to work, he meditated on a new scheme to make his life easier.

Gavin had a devious mind and was determined to develop a plan. He was often caught snooping in the Leonardville homes, creating a plan to steal items from the local residents, but no police reports were ever made. With Gavin the plan was sure to be diabolical and hurtful to many, so what could he steal?

Gavin's plan was put into action on the morning of December 14th, 1999, the day before the murder. Tom Ward had seen a small red car parked on the North Side of Barton Rd. While Tom was puzzled about the car's position, he also said that he didn't see the driver sitting in it.

That same morning, Travis Hegerty saw the same red car around 7:30 AM, although it was now located in the driveway of another neighbor. He remembered seeing the car with the headlights on but he did see someone sitting in the vehicle.

The car had fit the description of Gavin's vehicle and his MO of scouting for things he could steal. The question was to find where Gavin's car is now. Is there any evidence from the murder in the car? Determining this information was a priority to move things forward. Detective White didn't fully understand why the Stumpp residence would be of interest to Gavin.

Detective White then went to the DMV and searched through the list to find a link that would connect the vehicle to the Stumpp's. Unfortunately, there were way too many vehicles to get a quick answer.

White knew he had to look for a red car in Marion's parents' name. Years had passed since the vehicle was purchased, and Marion rarely had the car in her possession. Somehow, she had a tough time remembering the red car was purchased through her parents. She didn't even remember if they still had it when the baby was born.

"We drove the car to Arkansas shortly after December. Then we sold the car a few years later as a trade on another car", said Marion.

Detective White sat in his office reading through the documents from Marion, hoping to get a conclusive answer.

"Then where did it go from there?" Detective White muttered to himself the records were getting harder to track. He went through every record and every document. Finally, after a long search, he found that the car was sold directly from the dealership to an auction house in the Texas area, which then sold the car to a dealership in Mexico.

He was happy that he had found something to go on. Immediately, he called up a translator in the department and was able to make a call directly to the dealership in Mexico.

"Yes, we had purchased the car from the auction house, and that is all our records show. We can't find any records to show who purchased the car from us, and who might have it now," he said. That was all that was needed.

And that was the end of the trail. No evidence could be found from the car at this point.

Gavin had the right color car, the right style of car, and was driving in the area with the car during the time of the murder. It was all circumstantial but given what White knew it was enough to add another piece to the puzzle.

✪   ✪   ✪

THE BOOT

On the cold morning of the Stumpp murder, snow- covered the areas. With that assistance, the detectives were able to draw out many observations outside the crime scene. Where did the murderer come from? In which direction did he go? What type of shoes was he wearing?

With no answers still, the detectives were ready to be creative with their thought process. Det. Rhino was hoping for the slightest hint of progress and was interested in any notification that brought them closer to the crime scene. Recently a new set of tracks had been identified. Before Rhino could draw his conclusion and solve the case he needed to find answers to why Gavin was waiting on the North Side of the property, as evidenced by the pacing back and forth in the snow. Perhaps he wasn't ready with the courage to be a cold-blooded murderer.

The front door was blocked by the decorated Christmas tree and the discovered tracks lead to the side door where Olive would have invited the suspect into her home. The detectives knew Gavin had already introduced himself as her customer only a month ago. If he had then come to her with an elaborate story of a broken-down car, she wouldn't hesitate to help him out. Nothing seemed as out of the ordinary as it should have been.

It was quite out of character for Olive to come to the door dressed as she was. According to her husband, she always looked presentable when answering the door, no matter what time it was.

One would expect that Gavin would have exited the house the same way as he had entered. It was all being laid out in plain sight as the tracks left from the side door.

There was no doubt in anyone's mind that Det. Rhino had more CSI experience than any other officer in the department. Many thought Det. Rhino could paint the picture of the crime inside his head and imagine himself walking through it.

He always felt like a man on a crusade when it came to solving a crime. Both Det. Rhino and Det. White were part of a special group of investigators that helped other agencies with their investigations. Det. Rhino could get inside the mind of a killer and know exactly how the evidence fit the crime.

What intrigued the detectives most was the impeccable clarity of the footprints found. All of the details were visible. The boot print was the single best evidence they had at this point, and it could easily pay off. It did not take much effort to distinguish the brand name and size. The detectives were also able to discover it was a size 8 Northwest Territories hiking boot, primarily sold by K-Mart. Since most popular men had a shoe size between 10-12 in Kansas, it was pretty easy to narrow down the list.

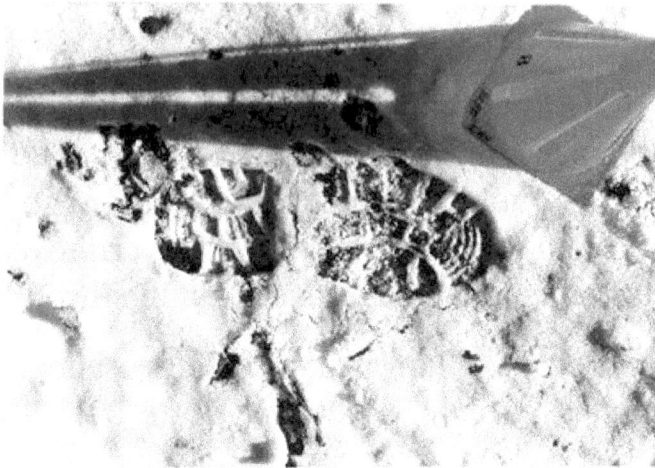

Gavin was 5 foot and 8 inches, which meant he had smaller feet. Since the odds were in their favor, they were able to search his house for the shoes. Excited to see what they would find; the investigators made their way to his house to discover his shoe size was 8.5. The investigators did not back down since it is not unusual to have slightly different shoe sizes in different brands.

During their initial investigation, Det. Rhino was able to track the prints through the snow as they were leaving the Stumpp home on the Northside of the house, then turning towards the West across the neighbors' field before heading back to the south.

The footprints had gaps between them, so Det. Rhino concluded that the murderer must have been in a hurry. They continued examining the prints towards the south and across the road through another field before heading towards the east. It appeared the murderer made some effort to run the distance in the night as the footprints continued east across Barton Road and through the golf course, where the heat of the day had melted away the tracks.

Det. Ryan needed to prove his point about shoe sizes varying by manufacturer. To do that, he tried on the size eight boot found at K-Mart, which matched with the prints in the snow. After trying the boot on, Ryan was convinced that Gavin could have worn a size 8 boot. The Northwest Territories boot was a little loose, which could easily fit any person who wore a size 8.5 in other shoes. As the case progressed further, Detective White felt like Sherlock Holmes trying to solve the case. He was trying desperately to connect all the pieces.

As Marion persistently continued adding to her story, she retold how Gavin usually wore hiking-type boots because they were most comfortable. She also recalled they would shop at K-Mart pretty often but couldn't remember if they had brought the Northwest Territories boots there or not.

As the case was concluding, this was one piece of the puzzle that fit right into place. Since Gavin could easily fit the boot on his foot, all that was left to do was find his boots. The question was, where exactly could they be?

Maybe the boots were at the crime scene sitting at the golf course! Or they could be at either the neighbor's backfield or possibly at Marion's place. Marion had already permitted them to search the house, but the murder was three years ago. Detective White believed there was still a chance the boots could be laying there in the back of the closet, waiting to be found.

❂   ❂   ❂

THE WITNESS

Marion's son, Kevin Ruez, was 11 years old in December of 1999. During Marion's many interviews, she would speak about him. Marion also explained that Kevin was her son from a previous relationship living with his father in Santa Maria, Texas until 1999 when he started to live with her.

When she came in for one of her interviews, she began to explain some events of 1999. She told the detectives that Kevin had been living with her at Christmas. At that time, Gavin had purchased a satellite dish for his parents in Arkansas, and Kevin had insisted he wanted to go with him to install the dish. Although Marion didn't approve of this, Kevin was adamant. They had another lead, and it was someone Detective Black could easily find.

Black was able to track down Kevin in Texas, and with his father's permission, he could give an account of what he remembered about the trip to Arkansas or any other related events during 1999. It was time to proceed.

Det. Black and Det. White boarded a flight for Texas and landed in Brownsville, TX. The trip wasn't that exciting as both Det. Black and Det. White couldn't sleep during their flight. When they arrived in Santa Maria to talk to Kevin's father, the man was not happy to see them. The crime rate in Santa Maria was not much higher than Mexico but the people were unhappy with the economic conditions and the lack of facilities provided to them.

Kevin's father told them that Kevin was attending school in Mexico, which means that the interview would have to be conducted at his school. Det. Black didn't approve of this, but she had no choice. They checked in with the local police authorities in Santa Maria to explain their purpose of the visit. They were clearly instructed about how the interview with Kevin would be performed on the school premises. Det. White and Black were already aware that Santa Maria was a border town and that traffic from Texas into Mexico was very common.

It was obvious that the local police authorities from the United States were not welcome on the Mexico side of the border. They were also instructed to hide any money, jewelry, badges, and even their sidearm. They were only allowed to take a small camera to record the testimonial and a small notepad to write down important details.

Det. White didn't want to insult the local police authorities in Mexico since this was critical for them. He told Det. Black to cooperate with the school and do whatever was necessary.

The local authorities also explained the reason for hiding their cash away. It was customary for the Mexican border police to ask for a reentry fee into the USA from the American authorities.

Kevin's school was very accommodating, especially for the interview process to take place. The detectives would have all the privacy to themselves. It was also comforting to know that many American children were living in Santa Maria and attending the school in Mexico, which would also help as Det. Black or White didn't know how to speak Spanish.

Children wore school uniforms and were very polite and cooperative. As the detectives walked along the hallways of the school they were led by a teacher to a room where they could easily talk to Kevin in private.

As soon as Kevin came, the detectives explained who they were and why they needed his help to figure out if Gavin has indeed committed the murder. They also wanted Kevin to feel comfortable with them and speak the truth. Kevin was 14 years old and if he was comfortable with the detectives there was a lesser chance, he would lie to them.

Kevin sat on a seat while the teacher stood a short distance behind him to assure Kevin he was in good hands and didn't need to be afraid of the detectives; they were just doing their job. She also assured him that if he felt afraid or uncomfortable while talking to the detectives, then she would stop the interview right away. She would also translate if there appeared to be any language barriers.

As expected, Kevin was very polite when the detectives spoke to him. They had set up the camera and introduced everyone present in the room. Luckily, they got right into the information which they needed to determine Gavin's character.

Kevin clearly said that he didn't like his stepfather. He was meaner to him than he was with other people. He knew it might be because Kevin was not his real son, but after the baby was born, things became even worse than usual.

There were not many details on how Gavin was mean to him. Gavin did not hit him or abuse him, but the detectives insisted Kevin elaborate more about how Gavin was mean to him.

The relationship between Kevin and Gavin was very strained. Kevin told the detectives Gavin mostly yelled at him, made him do chores in the house or the yard, but what bothered him the most was that his stepdad tried to humiliate him by making him crawl around in the yard, pulling weeds.

The detectives asked specifically if he remembered anything from the trip to Arkansas since he was the one to insist on going with Gavin. Kevin then revealed he was instructed by Gavin to tell Marion that he wanted to go with Gavin and begged to accompany him. Kevin himself found that odd. Marion was then left to stay home with the baby.

However, the details regarding the trip were a bit sketchy for him as he remembered that they had taken a satellite TV dish with them to install at his parent's house. Kevin also said that Gavin didn't take anything along with him other than the dish itself. Even in Arkansas, he felt that the only reason why he was invited for the trip was to do all the heavy lifting.

Gavin had him prep the area for the TV dish and then dug a hole. Despite Kevin doing all the effort, Gavin still complained about how he was not doing it properly and taking so much time to do it. Kevin also said that Gavin was so mean to him that Grandpa Johnson had to step in and interfere, which made Kevin feel good that someone was standing up to Gavin.

When the detectives asked if there was anything Gavin may have left in Arkansas, Kevin said that there was an issue with his boots that made Gavin furiously mad.

Kevin shared that while Gavin was putting cement in the hole for the pole to secure the TV dish, he spilled some cement on his boots. Gavin threw the boots in the trash and was mad because he didn't have a second pair of shoes to wear back home. It almost seemed like he was glad to throw away the boots for some weird reason.

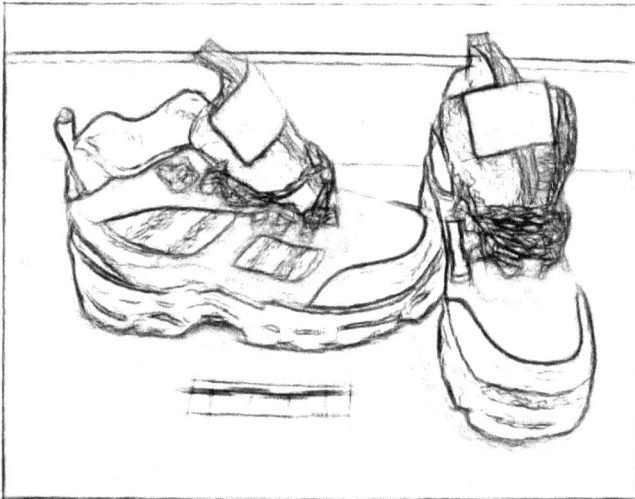

Kevin didn't remember a lot from the trip to Arkansas, but what he did remember was very interesting. Det. Black and White were starting to draw out important details from the interview.

Kevin never wanted to go to Arkansas, but Gavin insisted on taking him along and told him to lie about it. Gavin's boots were covered in cement and were thrown away in Arkansas. Gavin was happy about this.

These all fit with the timing of the murder, but what else did Gavin take to Arkansas? Yet another piece of the puzzle that needed to be fit.

They had to get back across the border before the Mexican police authorities figured out who they were and why they were there.

As the detectives made their way out of the school and down the street to blend in with the marketplace, they noticed salesmen coming from every direction. The vendors were hoping to catch their eyes to sell items to them. The detectives decided to buy a few things and gave the impression that they were tourists.

When they finally made it back to the Mexican border, all the border questions started to gain entry back into the States.

Who are you?

Where are you from?

What is the purpose of your visit? What are you taking back to the USA?

Let us see and inspect your camera. Wait, hold up, why did you take all these things?

Why were you visiting the marketplace? Why do both of you have notepads?

Because they were crossing at a busy time near the end of the day, there were still a lot of people lined up behind them. As the Mexican police authorities heard commotion from people behind them, they told them to move along. The detectives rushed to cross over to the U.S. side of the border.

Now, they were on to find the next missing piece of the puzzle.

THE GUN

Gavin's history with guns was not something surprising but was indeed suspicious.

Det. Black and White started to investigate Gavin's past background, determined to find the missing link of the puzzle. Both of them already knew the escape patterns that Gavin may have used to avoid being jailed. Most of the time, he got himself into trouble for forgery, bad checks, and scams. Gavin was quite the criminal, ensuring his tracks were not always evident. It wasn't until he got involved with Marion, did they manage to make his first connection with a gun.

As the detectives searched in-depth into his records, they got more suspicious. Gavin didn't function as a criminally insane person, not that they could see. It wasn't difficult to make a connection between the escalation in his behavior when they pulled up the dusty records from his military years.

"This looks interesting. What do you think, White," Det. Black asked, pointing out the image of the gun to him.

"Looks like we got a lead," He replied with a smile.

Det. Black continues, *"we need to go through everything again, every step Gavin took."*

We know in August of 1997, Gavin had waltzed into a famous pawn shop in Ogden, Kansas. Gavin looked up at the board which read, *"Pat's Pawn & Gun."*

He entered the pawnshop just outside the gates of Fort Riley, an Army Base. Once inside, Gavin looked over every gun, finally settling for a Ruger P95DC 9mm pistol.

As Det. White thought about it, a question popped in his head. *"Why did Gavin have the guts to shop for a gun like choosing an ice cream flavor at Ben and Jerry's?*

This evidence seemed odd. Was this the same type of pistol which was used in the Olive Stumpp murder? Could this be the evidence the detectives were looking for all along?

The records showed that Gavin had purchased a second gun too in December 1997, another Ruger P95DC. Where were these guns now? Why buy two of the same guns? The detectives knew that Gavin and Marion had several arguments in the past about having a gun in the house, but those arguments didn't happen until January 1999.

✪   ✪   ✪

The detectives reviewed the notes they had from Marion to make sense of it all. It was a known fact that Marion and Gavin had argued continuously if owning a gun was the right choice for protection in the house. Gavin was so angry about the gun issue at one point he showed Marion one of the guns which he had purchased without her knowing.

❂   ❂   ❂

From Marion:

As the cries of the argument turned towards fear and panic, Marion realized Gavin was capable of doing anything. The argument escalated to the level of pointing the gun towards her head without Gavin shaking or blinking an eye. This was a scary, dangerous moment for her.

Marion felt the coldness of the tip of the gun barrel where even its sound could be easily heard like a drumbeat.

"CLICK" The hammer fell towards this sound, and Marion quickly melted on the floor, starting to cry.

❂   ❂   ❂

Towards the end of 1999, Gavin began to spiral out of control as law enforcement was called during escalating arguments in the household. In the midst of this horrible drama, Marion conceived a child. In mid-February, the story started to spin out of control.

Was the pregnancy a consensual sexual encounter or rape? Was Marion still hoping Gavin possessed goodness in his deep dark heart, or was the pregnancy an outcome of rape, sexual manipulation, or fear during one of the many arguments?

In April of 1999, Gavin pulled over on the highway. He was arrested for a DUI while driving the Red Pontiac, which ironically connected him to the crime scene by the testimony of the witnesses on the day of the murder.

What had he been doing out on the country road at 3 am? There were no bars or known friends anywhere near where he had been pulled over.

It was clear that Gavin was turning his attention towards others and developing an infatuation with his KFC co-workers. He could easily get a hooker for the night, but he preferred to get close to the women and have more of a relationship with each of his co-workers. He decided to stalk the women all night, watching their moves, planning.

One evening in late July of 1999, Gavin wanted his co-worker, Dana, a blonde girl so badly he stalked her while she was out on a date. He waited for Dana to end her date and followed her to her apartment, where he forcibly raped her.

Detectives wondered if one of his purchased guns was involved as an intimidation to rape Dana. This was important because it would prove the point that Gavin could easily advance to killing with a gun if it met his motives.

Unfortunately, the victim never made a police report when it happened. Dana was not cooperating, and there were no other reports or statements to corroborate this rape. The detectives could use very little information about the incident connected to Gavin. Dana painted a picture of an escalating pattern of violence, said there were other victims besides her but couldn't provide names.

The detectives tried endlessly to find the identities of the victims, with every lead ending in a dead end.

There was still no information about the use of a gun. Everything Gavin did was somehow connected to the end murder, but the detectives still were trying to understand, how and the motive.

✪ ✪ ✪

Three years had passed since the time of the events without any knowledge or details of the victims. It could also be that the victims had already moved on with the new management. It seemed possible Gavin might have silenced them with a threat to never speak about the incident to anyone.

Gavin continued to wreak havoc in his home, abusing Marion and breaking things. Domestic violence was an everyday occurrence.

The police responded to the neighbors' complaint and arrived at their home in September 1999. This time an arrest was made when Gavin was found in possession of marijuana. To Marion's relief, Gavin spent five days in jail and received six months of probation. Unfortunately, within a few days of being released from the jail, the police were back at their house for yet another domestic violence complaint.

Alyssa was born on October 25th, which temporarily stopped the violence. Marion still hoped that Gavin would change his ways after Alyssa was born, but this was a foolish idea.

On Thursday, November 18th, 1999, Gavin drove to Leonardville Bank and opened an account in his and Marion's name, although he did not add her name on the signature card.

On Friday, November 19th, 1999, Gavin drove to Mr. Money Pawn in Manhattan, KS, where he pawned a Ruger P95DC 9mm pistol for $200.00. He took this money and traveled to the Leonardville Bank to make a $20.00 deposit in the account which he had opened just the day before.

This was very mysterious and led to many questions. What was the reason for his dealings at the bank, and how did this relate to employee Olive Stumpp? The answers were not clear and not enough for Det. Black and White to directly connect Gavin to the murder. Nothing was as simple as it seemed.

Gavin quit the Schwan's delivery service with a route in the Leonardville area after Alyssa was born. On Tuesday, November 23rd, 1999, Gavin returned to the Leonardville Bank. This time, he withdrew his entire money and closed the account which he had opened only a few days earlier.

Tuesday, December 7th, 1999, just 14 days after his last visit to the bank, Gavin returned to the

Mr. Money Pawn Shop to retrieve his 9mm pistol. Eight days later, on Wednesday, December 15th, 1999, Olive Stumpp was found dead in her basement home in Leonardville, Kansas, from gunshot wounds consistent with a Ruger P95DC 9mm, according to the autopsy report. The same type of gun which Gavin bought back from the Mr. Money Pawn Shop.

Why would Gavin go back to get the same gun which he had pawned only a few days ago? Why did Gavin use the same gun instead of another one of his handguns from home?

December 17th, 1999, two days later, Gavin took Kevin to Arkansas to install a satellite TV dish for his parents. The investigation report confirmed that on December 18th, 1999, an account was also set up for Gavin's residence for TV service.

Two months later, Gavin returned to visit his parents' home in Arkansas again to allow his baby daughter to meet his parents.

"Where are these two Ruger 9mm guns?" Det. White asked.

"Did he take them to Arkansas?" Det. Black chimed in, deep in thought.

If he had taken the guns to Arkansas, could they be buried in the hole for the satellite dish and covered it up with cement?

On Monday, March 31st, 2003 Gavin confessed to shooting and killing Olive Stumpp while being drunk. This was also the time when violence was escalating between the couple to a point where Gavin was insanely beating up Marion.

Friday, April 18th, 2003, Gavin opened up a bank account at Leonardville Bank. Why would he do this, wondered Det. White. Was he revisiting the crime to relive the moments, to take pride in himself for getting away with murder? Perhaps he was planning on doing another crime as an extension of the murder. Who knew?

Questions seem to arise all the time. Was the plan to rob a bank from the beginning or was he a murderer in for the joy and thrill of killing, like when he killed critters in his youth.

By September 6th, 2003, Gavin and Marion had been fighting and arguing for six months straight. Many of the arguments were related to the fraudulent checks, scams, and forgery Gavin initiated. Although he was arrested and went to court to answer for all these petty crimes it would not lead to murdering someone with a gunshot. Even his parole officer was confused if he was a rapist, a murder, or possibly both.

To prove Gavin was the main suspect in the murder of Olive Stumpp, Det. White needed to find the guns, and one of them had to be the murder weapon.

If the detectives could find the guns, the case would be resolved. Det. White wanted Gavin to be punished and be accountable for the crimes that he had committed as soon as possible. Sharing the same air with Gavin was insulting, and he needed to be stopped and proven guilty.

"Why is he still breathing?" He kept asking this to himself as if his mind would give him a suitable answer. Only finding the murder weapon could answer that for him.

"It has to be Gavin; there was no one else who could fit the profile so perfectly."

As Detectives White and Black dug deeper into the never-ending well of records, they found a new pawn record that had not been reported to the police as of March 6th, 2003 at Wildcat Pawn for a Ruger P95DC 9mm gun, the gun was never redeemed after the pawn, and was subsequently sold.

"Are you sure? Are the records proper, or has anyone tampered with it?" Det. White was arguing with Det. Black.

The records showed the new owner of that Ruger P95DC 9mm pistol was a soldier who had been transferred for a station duty at Fort Drum, New York. As for her expertise in tracking and finding a needle in a haystack, Det. Black was able to track down the soldier, and he voluntarily took his gun to the local police station in the area. They took custody of the weapon and then sent it to the Riley County police for processing.

It was quite evident it had been logged and filed with all the appropriate paper records. The pistol was duly checked-in and preliminary; it came to be the same type of gun identified by the crime lab with the serial # xxx- x1076, which had matched the pawn records with the slip in 2003 at the Wildcat Pawn. Other pawn records from Pat's Pawn also showed that this gun, along with the second P95DC with the serial # xxx-x0033, could it be the same gun?

The question now was which gun was used or if Gavin could have purchased a second gun just in case to create confusion and elude the police.

Federal Drug fire test of the P95 xxx-x1076 gun, unfortunately, indicated that they had recovered the wrong gun. This was still the only piece of the puzzle that made sense to convict Gavin as the murderer. Both of them knew that all that was needed was to find the other gun to close the case and get a conviction.

THE SEARCH WARRANT

The trip to Mexico was not a complete bust, as Det. Black and White were able to pinpoint the amount of time Gavin needed to destroy evidence during his Arkansas trip to his parent's house. Now, all they needed to figure out was what else Gavin took to Arkansas. After learning the Arkansas trip took place just two days after the murder, they knew that the boots were likely thrown away. They needed to verify if the gun was still in Arkansas or not.

Det. Black, in a desperate attempt to learn more about the trip made to Arkansas, called Gavin's father.

"I would like to talk about your son, Gavin, and about the trip that he made to your home to install the satellite TV for you," Det. Black said.

The old man seemed very reluctant to talk about anything, but he was compliant with Det. Black's question. Det. Black had a way of persuading people to speak about the things which they didn't like to talk about.

Black asked if Gavin's dad remembered anything from Gavin's visit to install the satellite TV dish at their place. He recalled the event but didn't remember anything about the boots or the cement. He did say that the hole for the pole was not very deep.

"How do you know this?" Det. White asked him like an examiner at an entrance exam.

"The color of the cement indicates that not much was used to cover the hole." The old man replied hastily, almost complaining that his son had done a half-assed job.

Det. Black needed to determine if Gavin had buried the gun in the hole or not, so he asked him if he knew anything about a weapon Gavin could have brought here.

"Yes!" The old man replied without flinching. Det. Black quickly asked, *"where is it?"*

He replied that Gavin had already told him about the gun, and both Marion and Gavin had a fight, and she didn't want the gun to stay in their house since he had once put the gun to her forehead. He asked his dad to keep it for him at his home.

This was great. Finally, some real nice piece of evidence in this murder case except making assumptions. To Det. Black's hope, the gun was still in Arkansas, lying in wait for them to pick it up.

Det. Black quickly called White without wasting any time. She told him to prepare an affidavit for a search warrant in Arkansas, at Gavin's parents' home.

This was the first time Det. White ever asked for a search warrant in another state. It was not difficult for him to get a warrant. He was hesitant to search for a warrant in another state to avoid complications or go against duty protocol.

Arkansas was not a very big state, and the search warrant was not challenging to obtain. Arkansas had small-town folks with small-town ways, like an old farm town. The street next to his parent's home where Gavin grew up was named after his family.

Both Det. White and Det. Black learned getting the warrant prepared was the easy part, but getting it signed by a judge in Arkansas was much more difficult. They both knew that they had to make a few calls to their connections down at the Justice Department to get the judge to sign the search warrant.

Det. White knew since it was a small town, they would accept the paperwork requesting a search warrant, but it would not be signed unless both detectives were there in person to attest to the facts of the case and why they needed a search warrant of Gavin's parent's house in front of the judge.

Det. White knew even if he had to drive to Arkansas for the judge to sign some papers, and then he would do it. If he had to stay awake all night long driving to Arkansas, he would do it.

Det. White got in an unmarked patrol car to beat the traffic and drove straight to Arkansas. The police department had a policy that they were not supposed to drive for more than 8 hours in a single day. Det. White was becoming stressed to get to Arkansas as quickly as he could. Det. Black insisted that they should stop for the night and continue their journey in the morning to meet with the judge.

Since it was the middle of the night in an unfamiliar area, they had no option but to stop at the first available motel. Det. White parked his undercover car and went to the motel's front desk to ask for two single bedrooms. He discovered there was just one single room available in the small town. He agreed to the single room while looking shyly back at Det. Black.

They already knew that they had no option but to share one room. They were adults and Det. Black was regularly referred to as his work wife since he had spent so much time with her. Both of them agreed and went straight to bed with high hopes for tomorrow. Det.

White slept on the sofa with his back to the bed to give Det. Black some space to privately sleep on the bed.

They set the alarm to wake up early in the morning to leave for Arkansas. They were still behind on their attempted schedule.

In the morning, they quickly drove to meet the judge at his hometown in Dumas, Arkansas. Det. White made sure he had sufficient paperwork for the judge to issue a search warrant. He was thrilled to finally find the gun Gavin's father referred to, but more than that, he was hoping for a positive outcome to be done with this case and the guilty party sentenced.

When they arrived in Dumas, he called the Sheriff's Department office to quickly get a local officer assigned to assist them in their investigation. It was best to have the local law enforcement agency serve the warrant for the case.

Soon they were met at the judge's office by Deputy Duke, who appeared more Russian than American due to his mustache and bulging tummy. It was soon coming to an end.

"It's been a long time since I've had to deal with Gavin and his brother. I was hoping they had ended up in prison. I was certain their petty crime spree had been cut short almost 15 years ago," said Deputy Duke.

Deputy Duke drove with the detectives to the home recalling stories of mischief with Gavin and his brother. It was a beautiful morning when they left for the county and traveled on the long bumpy gravel road.

They approached the house and found the satellite dish positioned on the side of the house shining from far away. The trip had been beneficial to hear all the stories about the expeditions of Gavin and his brother.

Deputy Duke knocked on the door, and Mr. Johnson opened it. Detective Black as the lead, introduced herself and everyone with her since she had spoken to him previously.

"We have a search warrant for your house. We are looking for a gun that Gavin might have hidden here," Deputy said to Johnson.

"Well, hell, y'all drove all the way from Kansas just to hold this gun?" Johnson replied. *"Gavin*

was installing the satellite, and that was when he asked me to keep the gun with me. I have kept the gun under his bed in his old room – you can have it," Johnson added.

Mr. Johnson asked them to follow him, and he led the way to the old room where he had hidden the gun long ago. He pulled the gun out from under the bed as it was wrapped up with great care in a plastic Wal-Mart bag and handed it to the Deputy.

"Here you go, take it," said Mr. Johnson to Deputy.

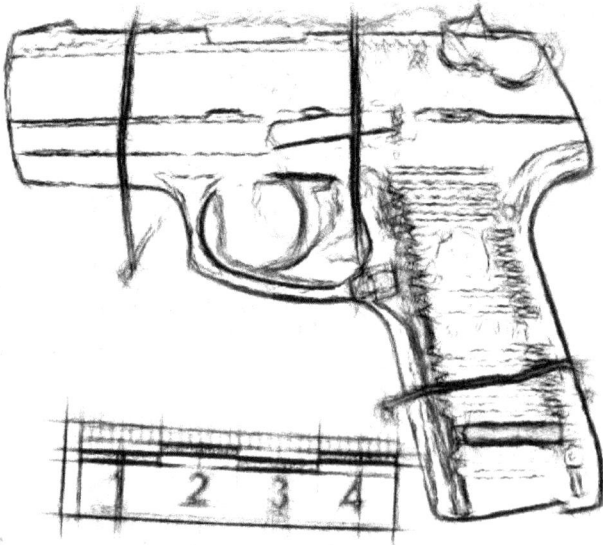

It was strange that Mr. Johnson willingly gave the gun to the Deputy without any questions. Why did Mr. Johnson never ask them the reason for retrieving the gun, or what Gavin might have done with the gun, or if he is aware that Gavin is locked up in Kansas?

Deputy Duke knew Mr. Johnson was a little gruff and had a direct personality. He also admired his simple way of living.

"We were all anxiously waiting to check the model and the serial number of the missing Ruger P95DC with the gun", said the Deputy. With careful handling Det. White peeled back the Wal-Mart bag and opened the box to check the details while holding a silent breath of excitement. It was a happy moment when the serial number matched, and the long detour wasn't for nothing.

The detectives took the evidence into custody after clicking some photographs for their record. *"Thank you for your cooperation,"* said Det. White to Mr. Johnson and Deputy Duke.

"This road will lead you straight to the highway, which would take you to the road leading to Kansas," said the Deputy to the detectives as they

were leaving the county. Deputy also made his final report of the proceedings in the execution of the search warrant and the findings.

This piece of the puzzle seemed to be an overwhelming answer, but the detectives were content with what they had achieved so far.

The detectives were in a remote area without cellular connections. Finally, a ray of hope for them came when they got connected to their cellular carrier again and could make the call to their Captain back home.

"We have retrieved the weapon that might have been employed at the crime scene," Det. Black told Captain Dubbs when she called into the Police Department.

"Hurry and come in," the captain said to Detective Rhino. *"You will want to hear this!"*

"Detectives, What a wonderful job! I recommend you to get to the forensic lab in Wichita for the comparisons of the bullets and casings. I just spoke to them, and they are waiting for your arrival," Detective Rhino instructed Det. Black and Det. White on the call.

It took a whole day of driving to reach the KBI lab in Wichita, KS. *"We can't stop as we have to reach the lab before they shut their doors,"* said Detective Black to Detective White despera*tely.* *"Finally, we made it here,"* the detectives exchanged words. Detective Black was leading the way, holding the evidence in her hands. The door opened, and they handed over the gun to the forensic team. *"Now we wait"* Det. White said as they left the premises to drive home amped on adrenaline, they ignored the 8-hour driving rule and drove straight home.

✪ ✪ ✪

Both the detectives returned to the police department, where they were congratulated upon their arrival.

"Welcome and congratulations, detectives. You both have done a good job," the Assistant Director of the Police Department said to the detectives as he called them both into his office.

"What were you both thinking?" the Assistant Director asked the detectives in an off tone. Both detectives looked at each other not sure what was meant by the comment.

"I just got the bill from the hotel you both stayed in, and the bill stated that you both rented only one room," said the assistant director to the detectives.

Both detectives laughed out loud at this statement and replied, *"What were we going to do? We are adults, and we were super tired, and it was all that was available at that moment. So, we rented the room without hesitation."*

"Is there anything I should be concerned about?" The assistant director asked both the detectives. Both detectives looked at each other's faces and laughed.

"Our friendship is professional, and there is nothing else to it." Detective Black blurted out.

"It has been 12 days since we gave the evidence to the lab, and we have yet to hear from them. What do you suggest? Should we call the lab for confirmation?" Detective Black and White talked to each other on October 27th, 2003.

Detective White called the lab for an update.

"Hello, this is Detective Black. My partner and I submitted evidence 12 days ago and have not received an update since then. Can you please let us know the status of the bullet comparison?" Detective White asked the lab's attendant.

"Sir, we cannot give you any update yet, but the findings from the proceedings should be available in a day or two," replied the attendant.

"Why aren't they giving us the information? What is taking them so long to identify the weapon and the bullets? I am not sure how to perceive the delay," said White. The detectives were visibly shaken.

They were not expecting the results they received from the lab.

"Hello, this is Chad from the Wichita lab. We have gotten the report from the evidence that you both submitted 13 days ago," the detectives on speakerphone were happy and anxious at the same time, listening to the verdict.

"I have good news to tell. The bullets are a perfect match with the bullets at the crime scene. So are the casings. It is now quite certain that this is the gun that killed Olive Stumpp," Chad said.

"Thank you for the update," replied detective Black. *"Det. White, we have clarity on this puzzle, and the picture now shows that Gavin deliberately killed Olive Stumpp,"* said Detective Black.

"You are right, Det. Black, but I have a different picture in my mind of the plan Gavin was executing. I'm convinced there is more to this story. I envision Gavin holding Olive Stumpp as a hostage to get into the bank and gain access to the vaults before anyone arrives at the bank that morning. It is obvious that Olive refused. Maybe he didn't know about her knee injury, and when she refused, Gavin acted out in rage as he had done with Marion in the past, but this time he had a loaded gun" said Detective White.

CHAPTER 11

THE TRIAL

Det. Black entered the halls of the courthouse, a large limestone building from the late 1800s. Signs hung in the halls instructing visitors to keep their voices down as the entire building with the stone walls and the vaulted coved ceilings sounded like an echo chamber. The hearing for the attempted murder was on the third floor, and the prisoners were brought up through a security elevator.

Det. Black stood in the hall waiting with Marion and the District Attorney Brenda Gordon as the doors to the elevator opened. "Crap" Brenda exclaimed as Gavin stepped out of the elevator. I was hoping we were seated in the courtroom before he got here.

"Marion", Gavin cried out, "Call my Mother. Let her know you got me arrested for attempted first-degree murder."

Det. Black stepped forward to block his view of Marion and told him he needed to be quiet, and he was not permitted to talk to Marion.

Gavin's response was heard all through the halls, *"Shut up bitch!"*

The correction officers were trying to move Gavin into the court, thinking the separation between him and the victim would calm him down.

His ranting continued, though as he was yelling *"you fucking cunt"* as he was being dragged away.

It sounded like the Grand Canyon as his final words hung in the air. Det. Black was not sure which of the three of them the final statements were for, but it was all heard by the presiding judge.

The tone was set for the hearing, Gavin with some help from his attorney, finally took his seat to answer the charges. The hearing took several hours—short for a case of this magnitude, but there were very few witnesses.

Detective Black laid out the elements of the crime and her testimony after the initial officers finished explaining their findings when they arrived at the home.

Det. Black painted a picture of a violent, manipulative, and controlling man. She also painted a very bleak picture of a broken woman in Marion. If there ever was a woman to show what "Battered Wife Syndrome" looked like it was Marion.

It seemed every 15 minutes, the judge was stopping the testimony to get Gavin under control. The technology advancement was not yet perfect enough to have him removed to watch from another room.

This was a preliminary hearing, not a trial, so no jurors were present. The goal was to determine if there was sufficient evidence to take the case to trial. So far, this was all just testimony from police officers on their observations of the home and statements taken during the investigation.

Gavin protested and was adamant that he was just trying to shut her up, not kill her. He had provided a statement shortly after his arrest which he testified that Marion was nagging him to the point he just wanted to hit her and knock her out. He had even confessed to a maintenance worker in the jail prior to his hearing.

The maintenance worker was working on the plumbing when Gavin struck up a conversation with him. Gavin had recognized him from KFC, where he had done some work on the walk-in freezer.

The worker asked innocently, *"what are you in here for?"* although he was not prepared for the response. Gavin seemed proud as he responded, *"Attempted Murder on my wife"*.

The worker, not sure how to respond, said *"what?"* Gavin explained that he had tried to kill his wife to shut her up because she was such a nagging bitch.

The worker finished as quickly as he could and went upstairs to the police administration building not knowing exactly who to tell, but he had to tell someone what just happened.

The worker was friends with many of the officers, and one let him into the investigation division to find someone to talk to. It was lunch, and most of them were out, except one. He worked his way around the division where all the cubicles were in the middle of the room until he came to one of the 4 private office sections.

First was the Investigation Captain. The door was closed with no one inside. Next, the Investigation Lieutenant, again, the door was closed with no one inside. Next, was the Drug Task Force Sergeant, and his door was always closed as they worked mostly nights. Last was an area in the corner with two large computer racks, a desk with 5 monitors spanning the six-foot desk, and another desk with two monitors like the rest of the detectives.

This was the Hi-Tech Crimes section and was situated so the five video screens were not visible to the rest of the office. The cases that were worked in this section were often children, and the horrible things people did to them. The worker poked his head in to see someone was working inside.

Det. White replied, "Hey, what brings you in here? "What did we break?" Mark, the maintenance worker, knew Brad, and he chuckled but then stopped as if he had seen a ghost.

Mark pointed at the monitor on the desk which was displaying a photo of Gavin Johnson. *"I just had a conversation with this man"*, he said.

He continued to explain how Gavin had confessed to him that he had tried to kill his wife to shut her up.

Even Gavin was silent in the courtroom as Mark explained his encounter. Here was a stranger he had confessed to, and now it was Det. White's turn to take the stand.

✪ ✪ ✪

Detective White came into the courtroom and set up the computer monitors with speakers in front of the judge and each attorney. He started by explaining how the officers were dispatched and sent to the wrong address. This could have resulted in Marion's death, but as it was, this was the amount of time needed to capture Gavin's confession in his own words on the 911 recording.

During the struggle, Marion had dialed 911 and dropped the phone on the floor. During the call, the sound was terrible which Det. White played for the court.

"As you can hear, there was an argument in the background, and little bits and pieces were able to be distinguished through the noise".

The Defense Attorney stood up and made a motion to NOT accept the recording into evidence.

"This is clearly an argument in which my client has given testimony collaborating, but the words spoken in this argument were indiscernible."

Ms. Gordon stood up to agree with the defense attorney. *"We cannot make out what was said on this recording, but please let my detective continue to explain before you rule on the recording."*

The judge said, *"I would like to hear what the detective has to say before I rule. Please continue, Detective",* he said as he looked at Det. White in the witness box.

"I agree that it is very difficult to clearly hear the words spoken", Det. White explained. "When I listen to this, it is very hard to understand what was said. This is why I took this recording, separated the voices from the background noise, and then increased the volume of the voices so they were at a discernible volume. Now let's play this again".

Just as he went to click the button, the defense attorney again stood up and objected to the manipulation of the audio. The judge asked Det. White if he added anything to the audio to which Det. White replied, NO.

"I only took away excessive noise so we could understand what was said", White replied.

The Judge replied, *"I'll allow it"*.

Now when the recording was played, the voices were clear and yelling words were exchanged with Gavin and Marion:

> (Marion) *"Why are you getting a bottle of Chloroform?"*
>
> (Gavin) *"I swear to god you're going to be out just like that".*
>
> (Gavin) *"After that, you're going to wake up in the fucking lake"*
>
> (Marion) *"Where did you get that bottle?"* (Marion) *"People are going to know about this"* (Gavin) *"You left and went to Junction City. You never came back."*

Det. White then continued his testimony into the search warrant of the family computer and Gavin's purchase of the chloroform to show it was a planned event. He had further evidence from the computer where he had planned to change his identity in an effort to disappear after the death of his wife.

With that, the judge again had to take a break as Gavin screamed, *"That's some MacGyver bullshit. You can't allow it."*

When the judge returned, he made a brief statement agreeing there was sufficient evidence that an attempt was made on Marion's life, and Gavin was the person who planned a strategy to kill her. Gavin Johnson would therefore be on trial with the charge of Attempted First Degree Murder.

The indictment was read, and the trial was set. Gavin was facing Attempted Murder on his wife now along with the Murder of Olive Stumpp.

Gavin was still professing his innocence. No one knew why. In a discussion with his attorney and the prosecutor, he was asked why he was fighting the charges with the amount of evidence looming over his head.

In the attempted murder case, it was obvious Gavin was the one on the 911 recording telling Marion he would knock her out with the chloroform and throw her in the lake to make it look like a suicide.

Det. White reviewed the evidence in his mind. In the murder case, we recovered the gun used and recovered it from Gavin's family home in Arkansas. The attorney said that his client is asking questions about Jimmy Niles. It was then the detectives were made aware that Gavin had copies of the police reports from discovery, and he was learning how the case had gone cold.

During the weeks before the trial, Gavin had been recruiting other inmates to send letters on his behalf. Marion was the target of most of his letters, trying to intimidate her to testify on his behalf.

The letters seemed like they were from a man with a split personality or possibly a textbook psychopathic killer. They were sweet and reminiscent of romantic times during their early dating. He was trying to manipulate her with kindness, although in the same letter, he would tell her she would have to look him in the eye face to face when he got out of jail with her testimony she was providing in court.

The investigation division received a strange anonymous letter prior to the trial. The letter was postmarked from Lincoln, Nebraska, without a return address and sent to the Riley County Police Investigations Unit.

The handwritten letter was a confession making fun of the police for arresting the wrong man for killing Olive Stumpp. The letter explained that Jimmy Niles was in fact the killer and that the person writing the letter was his accomplice.

As proof, the writer offered insight into the killing motive of revenge on the Stumpp family for issues created in the Leonardville community. Marvin was a womanizer, and Olive was a prude who was denying landowners loans to keep their family businesses alive. The writer continued to say that this was a collaborative effort from many of the citizens in the community, to which Jimmy Niles was hired to take out the root of the evil, Olive Stumpp.

The writer explained that he had been driving the car on the morning of the murder while Niles explained to him how he was going to frame the guy he bought the gun from.

The letter concluded by stating there was blood in the trunk of the car he was driving, and investigators would be able to figure out who he was and where the car was located.

The following day Marion was at the police department during one of her regular visits, more frazzled than normal, demanding to talk to Det. White.

Marion explained to the detectives that she was threatened by Gavin and was fearful of him getting out of jail. She explained that in a letter she received from Gavin, in violation of his restraining order, he told her that he was getting out of jail on bond. He demanded she helps him with his defense on the murder charge and drop the attempted murder case too.

She shared that Gavin was directing other inmate buddies presently out of jail to follow her. Marion was in fear of her life and her daughter's life. Other inmates were also mailing her letters from Gavin that said he was going to have her killed if she didn't help him.

Det. White immediately started a very unprecedented search warrant that was renewed every 3 days with the judge to intercept any and all mail which could be associated with the inmate Gavin Johnson.

The investigation started collecting mail immediately on the first day. Detectives found a letter from Gavin to his parents and letters to Marion. In the letters to his parents, he professed his innocence. Other letters were given to inmates who added them to letters to their families, who then mailed them to Marion. These were the more threatening letters telling her how to testify in court, but none threatening her life.

The letter Marion intercepted through another inmate gave instructions to pick up a letter stuck in the fence of the jail, in a location not easily watched by the guards. Gavin didn't have access to the yard. His one hour per day outside was in a courtyard simply to give him sunlight. The inmate who put the letter in the fence was convinced to do so to receive extra food from Gavin.

The detectives waited until late at night when no one would see what was going on in the yard. They retrieved the letter folded up and under a rock at a part of the fence just big enough to lift it and put the folder paper under.

The handwriting was the same as the anonymous letter previously received from Nebraska. This letter, according to the instructions, was meant to be sent from Nebraska. In this letter, the writer accused the police of ignoring him, and he had more evidence to show that Jimmy Niles was the killer and that several wealthy businessmen in Leonardville had financed the killing to get other business projects approved and past Olive Stumpp.

The writer also explained how Niles told him that he had given the murder weapon back to the guy he bought it from and had left tips with his wife, Marion about killing a woman in Leonardville, hoping she would tell the police.

Det. White now had the new letters in hand and compared the handwriting and other factors of the letters. As expected, the handwriting was the same as the letters being sent to Gavin's parents, which he had no reason to deny. In those letters, Gavin was mostly professing his innocence and asking for more money on his commissary account to pay off jail debts. The extra money he needed was probably needed for the food he was using to pay his fellow inmates to mail letters.

The detectives confronted Marion about the letters from Nebraska. She began to cry like she always did, but this time she was also apologizing. She explained that she was so fearful of Gavin getting out of jail that she had to mail the letter to show him she was helping, and he would not kill her.

When Det. White tried to explain how Gavin's bond was set so high that he was not going to be able to bond out even if his parents put up the family farm, Marion's only response was *"You don't understand"*.

After 10-15 minutes, the detectives were able to get her calmed down enough to explain why she was so scared. Gavin had issued a HIT on her life if she didn't help him.

Marion explained that she had only mailed the one letter, and any others would have been mailed by the inmates working for him.

From these letters, additional charges were added to the growing case against Gavin. Now with the addition of Violating a Court order of "no contact" it would be Witness Intimidation and additional Criminal Threats.

✪   ✪   ✪

Weeks later, in what almost seemed like a secret meeting, the court reconvened, and this time Gavin was seated in total silence, with no audience to play to in the courtroom.

Ultimately a plea agreement of 16 years was made in the Attempted Murder.

✪   ✪   ✪

"What was his play?", Det. White was thinking, why this change in demeanor and a lack of fight. It was only a matter of one day before he was presented with at least part of his answer.

With the new charges being presented, the defense attorney was trying to use his leverage of knowing Gavin was going to jail to his advantage.

The defense attorney was coming forward with the assertion the wrong person was in jail for the murder of Olive Stumpp. Even with the evidence in these new charges, Gavin was trying to fabricate an alibi and create a secondary suspect in Jimmy Niles. He explained that his client was spending days reading the case files and the leads on Jimmy Niles were correct. Gavin claimed that he had sold the gun to Jimmy Niles. The day before he took his trip to Arkansas, Niles had contacted him to return the gun saying he didn't like it.

Gavin, in true form, claimed that he only gave back half the money for the gun and that he left it in Arkansas because he knew Marion didn't want it in the house with the baby.

✪ ✪ ✪

Gavin was looking at the hard 40 in addition to the 16 years he had just been handed from trying to kill Marion.

The following month the Stumpp family found themselves in court, now witnessing the actions and antics of this deranged killer firsthand. When the court was finally settled the judge proceeded to announce that the defense wished to make a change in the plea in the case of Olive Stumpp's murder.

STATEMENT OF FACTS

(Statement read at plea hearing by the prosecutor)

(Full Statement of Fact as read in open court is detailed in Appendix 1)

"Madam Prosecutor, you may read your Statement of the Fact that you wish to present to the court in lieu of witness testimony", said the judge. The prosecutor started to explain who Olive Stumpp was and how her morning went on the day of her death, walking the court through the details before shifting to Marvin. She sighed for a moment before she walked the court through his discovery of the woman, he had spent his entire adult life with. Her statement detailed the investigation, the statements from the witnesses who placed Gavin's vehicle on the country road as he stalked his victim. She speculated that the ultimate goal was to rob the bank, that somehow in Gavin's mind, he would be able to get Olive Stumpp to take him to the bank before it opened and access the vault to commit the robbery.

The judge and gallery in the court hung on every word while Gavin's look of disgust grew with each detail. Gavin's attorney looked like a desperate homeowner trying to wrestle with his dog, holding his muzzle shut, so he didn't bite the neighbor.

Detail after detail, she walked her captive audience through the investigation linking the witness statements and the police investigation's findings together. All of this links to the drunken confession given by Gavin to Marion, with details never released to the public.

In the end, the gallery was left in tears and disgust for the crimes they were now privy to. The outburst from Gavin was not able to be contained by the attorney any longer, and with the help from the bailiff and two other officers in the court for added security, Gavin was moved to a chamber office.

The scene of overturned chairs and papers flung in all directions was slowly cleaned up by the attorney who was burdened with Gavin's defense. How can an attorney sleep at night after defending such a monster? We knew there were details from Gavin's mind that he shared with the attorney in an effort to make him believe the possibility of his innocence. Those same details also showed the attorney the insight of just how much of a monster he was sitting next to and what he was capable of doing in his fits of anger.

Just short of a scene from Hanibal Lector, Gavin was brought back into the courtroom and seated at the defense table, but this time with two officers directly behind him poised to pounce at the first sign of another uprising.

CHAPTER 12

CASE CLOSED

"This is Jennifer Speidel with Channel 5 KSNT News with a special report live from the Riley County District Court House."

"I am here today for this special report as the court hearing of Gavin Johnson has just concluded. We are hoping to bring you some live exclusive interviews with the judge, investigators, witnesses, and maybe even a word from Gavin Johnson himself."

"This story is about a killer who plotted and premeditated his strategy for killing an innocent woman, Olive Stumpp. While in court today I witnessed the proceedings and the evidence the prosecutors presented. In a last-minute *decision, Gavin Johnson changed his plea to NO CONTEST in an effort to get a chance at an appeal, and a lesser sentence."*

"The judge read off the charges;

- In the case 99-CR-35632, murder in the 1st degree of Olive Stumpp.
- In the case 03-CR-6722, attempted murder in the 1st degree of Marion Johnson.
- In the case 03-CR-7495, impersonation of a police officer Detective Gregory.
- In the case 03-CR-7868, intimidation of a witness, Marion Johnson.

After reading the charges, the judge ordered Gavin Johnson to stand.

In the cases of the attempted murder of Marion Johnson, the impersonation of a police officer, Detective Gregory, and the intimidation of a witness, Marion Johnson, the Defense had made a plea agreement. This court finds this agreement acceptable, and the Defendant is hereby sentenced to 16 years in the state correctional facility.

Now, as to the murder of Olive Stumpp, "How do you Plea?" Gavin muttered under his breath and was then nudged by his attorney to answer. In a soft, almost meek voice, he answered, *"No Contest"*.

Ms. Speidel continued her reporting. *"With a plea of No Contest the judge asked to hear the evidence from witness statements in the form of an affidavit of fact from the prosecutor."*

"Ms. Gordon finished her presentation with explicit facts from the key witnesses including detectives, neighbors, law enforcement, and family members for each of the crimes presented to the court." Here is Ms. Gordon now.

"Ms. Gordon, how do you feel about the outcome of the case, "the hard 40" Years on the Stumpp murder, and 16 for the attempted murder", asked Jennifer Speidel.

"I am pleased with the relentless investigation which brought us here today. Kansas is a state with no death penalty. The judge made the next best penalty of the Hard 40, *which means it will be 2044 before Gavin Johnson is eligible for parole for murdering Olive Stumpp. In 2044 he would then start his consecutive sentence for the attempt on Marion's life for the next 16 years. We will not be seeing or hearing anything else from Gavin Johnson until he is 95 years old,"* said Ms. Gordon.

The reporter shifted. *"Detective Black, may we have a brief moment to ask you a few questions?"* She pursued the detective, blocking her path.

Det. Black made eye contact with the Chief of Police as she received an approving nod to move forward with the reporter. In general, the detectives were discouraged from speaking to the media.

"Detective, as the senior officer in this second phase of the cold case investigation, what about this case would you have done differently?"

She replied, *"I don't know that I would have done anything differently as the evidence unfolded after Gavin attempted to kill Marion for her knowledge of the Stumpp murder."*

She continued. *"Marion is a woman who will need some help over the years for the damage Gavin has done. I am very proud of my fellow officers who helped us look through the consistent emotional statements from her to find the pieces we needed to make the link to the Stumpp murder."*

"My partner, Detective White, and I spent a lot of hours sifting through 3 years of cold case investigation notes to piece together the links. I'm glad we were able to give the Stumpp family the closure they deserved."

"Would you have done anything differently?"

Detective Black replied, *"My only wish is that we might have moved along faster with the case if Detective White had been involved with the original investigation. He has a unique way of looking through the leads".*

Marion came into view walking down the courthouse steps.

"Marion, can I ask you a few questions?" The camera moved in front of Marion Johnson.

"Marion, how do you feel about the outcome of your case?"

Marion was obviously shaken and trembling, with tears running down her face.

"I just hope he never gets out. He is going to kill me!" Ms. Gordon then pulled Marion away to end the questions.

"Detective White, could we ask you a few questions?"

The detective looked at the chief for his approval but only made eye contact with the Investigations Captain, who was shaking his head in disapproval.

Detective White replied, *"Sadly, I am unable to provide a comment at this time"*.

White glanced at the captain, *"I am needed on another murder trial"*.

This spurred the curiosity of the reporter. Was White working on another high-profile case? Was the arrest and conviction of Gavin Johnson connected to another murder that occurred in 2003?

The crowd disbanded, and Jennifer Speidel was left standing next to a fellow reporter, Logan Tyler.

He looked at Ms. Speidel, a renowned journalist, with frustration in his eyes. Logan said, *"At least you got a few interviews out of it."*

Logan was struggling to get off the mundane role of clerk for the local Manhattan Mercury, reporting on lost dogs, obituaries, anniversary announcements, and births in the hospital. All vital information for the Mercury to increase readership in the community, but Logan wanted to do investigative work. He had questions about this murder case, so many questions.

✪ ✪ ✪

Why didn't Marion go to the police sooner with all the abuse Gavin was subjecting her to almost daily?

Why did it take 5 years for the detectives to close the case when there were so many hints that Gavin was their perpetrator?

What is the real story of Kevin, Marion's son? Why didn't he live with Marion instead of living in Texas and going to school in Mexico? Logan said that he had seen a brief glimpse of a kid in the courtroom. Could that have been Kevin? He is only 16, and he disappeared as soon as the courtroom doors opened.

✪ ✪ ✪

Detective Black and Detective White were certainly relieved to solve the case, but they too had questions. They both had a gut feeling that Gavin Johnson committed the crime when records showed him opening a bank account in November of 1999 with Olive Stumpp at the Leonardville State Bank to close it days later.

Then there is the question of Marion Johnson.

Marion told a very decisive story almost daily of the abuse she encountered both physically and verbally from her husband, Gavin. The police heard stories continuously for years from Marion, but it wasn't until 2003 Marion came back to the detectives with new information of the exact details of the crime on Ms. Stumpp. She had been threatened by Gavin that he would do the same to her if she ever revealed the details to anyone.

It was a tragic, senseless murder of an innocent banker in a small town. Lives changed forever over money.

✪   ✪   ✪

Logan wanted to know more about Kevin, Marion's son, and how he was connected to the bigger story.

Kevin Ruez, the stepson of Gavin Johnson, may know more information than what the detectives originally thought. Logan Tyler had a week of vacation coming to him and decided he was going to take a road trip to Texas to learn this young man's story, now a 16-year-old. This could be the break Logan needed to get into investigative reporting.

✪   ✪   ✪

CHAPTER 13

BAD SEED

H is plane touched down in Brownsville, Texas. "Well, this is as close as I can get", Logan thought. "Damn it is muggy here too!"

Logan had many thoughts, *"Post 9/11 airport security is making the trip last forever. I'm instantly sweating as soon as I get off the plane. I would have moved to Kansas too if I lived here with this heat!"* These were just some of the things distracting him from the purpose of his trip. *"South Padre Island is close by, maybe I can take a detour to the beach and see what positive things there are in Texas, the beach sounds nice."*

Unfortunately, I only have a short vacation allotment of time to learn about Kevin and how he fit into the murder his stepfather committed. Thirty-Two miles to the border town of Santa Maria, Texas, population 578 this should be interesting.

✪ ✪ ✪

As a good reporter he broke, out his handy recorder; Kevin Ruez was born on Jan 10, 1988, in Santa Maria, Texas. He was one of the few witnesses in the murder trial for Olive Stumpp and was able to place the killer Gavin Johnson in Arkansas where the murder weapon was found.

Logan, in his research, found the address and names of Kevin's relatives in Santa Maria to find out more.

Kevin was a picture of a perfect little boy who had a deep respect for his Abuelita and the flip-flop she used for discipline. His parents didn't last long as a couple. His father was of Mexican nationality, and without official papers, was finding it hard to find quality work. He took these frustrations out on young Kevin and his mother, Marion. He was not physically abusive with them but very verbally abusive in the manner he spoke to them, which is why Kevin sought the protection of his Abuelita, the one person his father would never cross.

Life in Santa Maria was simple. He and his friends all grew up taunting the chickens and selling fruit until they were able to go to school. Once they started school, it didn't take too long before Abuelita insisted that young Kevin go to school in Mexico. The American schools were not teaching him his heritage, and since he was half gringo, the other boys picked on him and his quiet nature.

Kevin would walk to the school in Mexico with Abuelita every morning. Abuelita had a Texas driver's license and had several friends with the US government when she was young. They helped her get her official documentation papers and arranged for her to live in the US to keep her out of harm's way.

Kevin never really knew what Abuelita did with the government; perhaps it was just a story. Santa Maria was a border town and was one of the towns where there was a bridge over the river to Mexico and La Palma, where he went to school.

La Palma was a tourist town, with dozens of shops selling blankets, jewelry, food, and even puppies, with a large church, and a school guarded by men who only allowed the children and the nuns inside.

Kevin made many friends in Mexico, and most of them were jealous of Kevin because he went home to America every night. They would ask him to bring them things from America, cheap American or, should I say, Chinese toys mostly. Either way, it made him popular.

The school insisted that the students wear uniforms. Girls wore navy blue skirts, white socks, and a white blouse. The boys wore navy blue pants and a white collared shirt. Some even wore a red tie. There was no deviation from the uniform until they were outside the walls of the school.

Kevin became more popular when he discovered a cigarette machine at the market in Santa Maria.

His friends would give him money to buy the American cigarettes, which made them all look cool.

I learned that Kevin had moved to Kansas for the Summer with his mom when he was 10 years old to get away from his abusive dad. That was when he met Gavin. Gavin was the influence that would ultimately turn Kevin to the dark evil side. Ultimately Gavin sent Kevin back to Santa Maria when he was getting in the way of the planning and scheming of his forgery crime spree.

Kevin was 12 years old when Abuelita stopped walking him across the bridge, her health was fading, and the walk was just too much for her to do every day.

The visit from the American Detectives was a changing point for Kevin at 14 years of age. He had stayed under the radar of the gangs in Mexico, going home to Santa Maria every night. Kevin was a sweet boy until the gangs discovered his scent.

✪ ✪ ✪

Kevin was recruited for the Mexican cartel gangs as "new blood" when they noticed him crossing the bridge to go to the Catholic school in Mexico.

It started with them giving him $100.00 just to carry a small package back home across the border to Santa Maria, where he gave it to a man he was told was his uncle.

WOW! $100.00 was more cash than he had ever seen, and he had no idea how to spend it. Christmas was coming, and being the innocent soul, he bought gifts for his Abuelita, family, and extra food for the holidays.

Abuelita questioned him about the money and suspected the evil from the drug gangs. She chased him with that flip-flop for a week until he told her about the uncle he didn't know.

By then, the new friends in Mexico introduced him to the taste of Methamphetamine (meth) as part of his payment for carrying packages home from school. They gave him a variety of crystal meth that looked like candy "pop rocks".

As he got older, Kevin began using more meth. He was taking more meth as a form of payment than money for the over-the-border trips, and his behavior became worse. He was increasingly lying to Abuelita and stealing. He spent more and more time in Mexico with his new "friends" who influenced these actions.

His father at this point, was coming to terms with his anger through the help of the church and the dying wishes of Abuelita but couldn't get Kevin to go with him to the church to get him away from the new friends.

Kevin was learning many bad ways that scared him from the gang. The Mexican cartel often used machetes to behead people they captured who interfered with their business. Hostages were taken, bodies dismembered, all to maintain control over the townspeople and the cartel members themselves. It was getting scary for Kevin. Kevin was ready to move home and live with his mother in Kansas to get away from this before it killed him.

At 16, when the trial in Kansas was over, Kevin's father sent Kevin back to live with his mother, who was now raising Alyssia by herself and a mere shell of a woman she once was.

Logan returning from Santa Maria, brought his story to the Mercury editor about this troubled youth living in the house of a murderer and his drug-fueled life in Mexico.

The editor read through it, almost skimming the story. "It just doesn't have what we are looking for, Logan, no hook, nothing to grab the audience and pull them in," The editor commented. Logan didn't give up on his story but filed it away, adding notes of Kevin's crimes that made it into the police blotter, but the editor was right. It was just a sob story about a kid with a shitty life.

CHAPTER 14

CIRCLE OF VIOLENCE

Kevin's life as a sixteen-year-old in Kansas started off exactly how he wanted it to be. His mother was a basket case of emotions living day to day, doing her best to keep everything together. Kevin spent his time running the streets, making new friends, and enjoying country life in Kansas. It was a far cry from the drug lord living in the Mexican border town.

Kevin turned from trafficking drugs at the direction of the cartel to no parental direction or support at all. He wanted the money he was earning from his efforts from the Cartel, but in Kansas it was just not the same. Kevin found himself unknowingly following the steps of his stepfather, Gavin, committing small thefts from unlocked cars or stealing anything he thought he could sell to his friends or a pawn shop.

Det. White should have seen the pattern forming when he saw Kevin's name appearing daily in the blotter reports of crimes or just reports of suspicious behavior. He really should have seen something in Kevin's eyes on that dark foggy Spring morning one year after Kevin had moved to Kansas.

Kevin had shown up at a crime scene just a few blocks from his mother's trailer. Det. White had been called to a trailer where a 22-year-old man was trying to make it living on his own.

Charles Phillips was a good student from Manhattan High School who had, like so many, gotten hired at the Footlocker Distribution Center in Junction City after his graduation. It was a great job for a young man to make decent money, but the downfall was that he was still living in Manhattan, almost 30 miles away. He stayed in Manhattan because his girlfriend Julie was attending Kansas State University, and she needed to get to classes early, so his commute was the price he paid for a pretty girl.

Julie had called 911 when she had come home from class and saw that Charles' car was still in the driveway. She called, not because he was home, but what she found inside. Their trailer had very little furnishings as a young couple starting a life, but when she entered the trailer, the last thing she expected to see was her boyfriend hanging from the ceiling fan with an overturned chair at his feet.

The only clue left was a vague note in Charles' hand *"I'm Sorry"*. Julie could not shed any light on what Charles was sorry for, and the case was closed as the apparent suicide that it was.

What did Detective White miss from this case? Why was Kevin at the crime scene? He lived only a few blocks away but was there a tie to his being there? As it was, this question failed to present itself at the time, but maybe if it had, things might have ended differently for Kevin.

Kevin was 18 years old, still living at home with his mother and trying desperately to get a good job. Kevin is trying to make his mother and Alyssia happy in their little trailer of past misery. Of all the places, Kevin gets hired at KFC not even knowing that his mother and Gavin had worked there previously.

Currently Det. White continued to work the major crimes in cooperation with the case detectives trying to find the obscure forensic links otherwise missed.

Times were rapidly changing with detective work. The boots on the ground detective work was starting to give way to a younger crowd of police officers with different ways of doing things. Even the chain of command was changing. For so many years, Detectives worked as independents tapping into those years of knowledge and following their gut instincts.

Detective White had changed lieutenants in the investigations division a few times since becoming a detective. Lt. Jay was easily the Lieutenant who did his best to keep White's loose cannon attitude in check. Lt. Jay helped White stay focused on finding an end to the cases while letting go of those which would go unsolved.

After Lt. Jay was Lt. Hank who Det. White had known for many years, even dating back to when they both worked narcotics together: Det. White in Junction City, and then Det. Hank in Manhattan.

Hank was most concerned with keeping a close eye on Det. White as he developed the Hi-Tech

Crimes Unit. He had White move his desk into a corner where others could not see his screens.

Hank's concerns were repeated weekly as he asked how Brad was able to work those cases involving innocent liberties with children without going insane.

Det. White's answers were always the same. *"I don't see children when I am working the case" "I see evidence, and I focus my efforts on making the connection to the offender" "The day I start to see the cases as children, you will find me in a corner crying".*

This last move in the investigation division shakeup was one Det. White never wanted to see.

Det. White had a champion in the Division in Captain Dubbs, a Naval veteran with a knack for leadership. His directions were simple, *"Make me look good", "Make me proud"* and when we followed these rules, he ALWAYS had our backs. When we made a major arrest, it was a division effort, and the Captain took the credit, he then shared the credit when he made his press release. This is how he liked it, and we were happy to give him the job because when things went bad, he was also there to make sure it didn't come down on us.

It was his division and his responsibility. To this day, I know I would never have been able to make the cases I made without his leadership to develop the Hi-tech Crime Unit. Those days of great leaders came to an end when the overly educated & under-experienced were promoted.

Times are different. Now it is all about case clearance and not crime-solving. I would like to apologize if you have ever had a crime against you go unsolved. It may be because law enforcement has changed the goal to, Clear/Close minor cases solved or not!

In the investigations division there was a new captain, and he was all about case clearance, and not solving crimes. His efforts were to push out the old guard to make way for his select officer. Yes, men with the same goals.

Det. White continued to work his cases without regard to clearing cases, but as expected this will be his undoing.

It was a typical day in the investigations division when a friend of the family came into the police department asking for Det. White. White overheard and walked to the front desk to see who was asking for him since he hadn't scheduled any interviews. He found his estranged friends at the counter with a desperate look on their faces. It had been a few years since they talked as their respective kids had an issue that spiraled out of their control, and in the end, no one was talking. Now Det. White finds them at the counter needing his help, and the issues of the past are all forgotten in an instant.

Det. White learned that their oldest daughter had gone missing, and they had no clue or whereabouts of who she was with when she went missing. White brought in two other detectives to work the initial case while he did what he did best and chased the forensics.

Shelly was now in high school and had all new friends from when he had known her, but the pattern is usually the same. It was someone she knew that she left with or ran away with. The detectives went through the details of their life and Shelly's life while Det. White started looking for a way to track her.

Shelly now has a burner phone since her parents regulated her regular phone. It was only by accident that the detectives learned about this second phone since her regular phone was left at home as directed when she was in school. MHS did not allow cell phones in the school since they had experienced several incidents with students taking inappropriate pictures and sharing them, unknowingly creating child pornography. At this point, it was about educating them about what they had done and not prosecution.

Through Shelly's friends, detectives were able to learn the phone number on the burner phone she had obtained. Det. White did what he does and created a timeline of calls & events that were explained by her friends and family about a new boyfriend in her life. None seem to know this new boyfriend's name, but Shelly was consumed by him and began to distance herself from everyone, even her younger sisters.

She had planned to run away with him, and with the information on the new phone, they could see who she had been talking with prior to her disappearance.

Her parents were horrified when they learned a friend, she had known most of their lives may have been who Shelly had left with and was last speaking with her.

For the purpose of this story, we will just refer to him as the perp, as he doesn't deserve a name.

Det. White knew him and had met the perp on several occasions with Shelly's family. The perp had even lived with them for a period of time, but the girls never indicated or insinuated that he was weird or a pervert to give anyone any reason to question his connection to the girls.

The perp created a deeper connection to Shelly, 15 years his junior. Shelly never shared their age difference with anyone, what their connection was, or what this new boyfriend was talking to her about. Everyone was in the dark.

Det. White knew the clock was ticking. When she didn't come home from school, Shelly disappeared technically, but they quickly learned that she never made it to school.

Her parents, armed with new knowledge about the perp, were furious and said that the perp had left town a few years earlier and had not heard much from him except an occasional phone call. The only lead they could provide was that he had moved back home, which was somewhere in the South. Mississippi, Georgia, or Alabama, they really didn't know where.

Det. White started by tracking Shelly's new phone and showing the calls on the timeline leading up to her running. It seemed the conversations started on her regular phone 6 months previously with calls late at night for about an hour each time with Shelly taking advantage of the free nights calling to avoid creating a bill making her parents suspicious.

It wasn't long after the calls stopped on this phone and started on the new phone with the same amount of frequency until the past two weeks. At this point, Shelly was talking to him several times a day. The calls stopped the morning she went missing.

Thirty-Six hours, where could she be? We got a late start in looking since the phone was unknown, and Shelly was so secretive about everything in the past few months.

Cellular technology was striving forward with increased opportunities to connect with the world to enable law enforcement to track criminal behavior.

A list of all the calls on the new phone was obtained with a search warrant with information describing the method of calling. Every time a call is made, it is connected to a cellular tower to hand the call off to the phone service. There are a series of antennas on every tower that point in a specific direction, so when the phone connects to the tower, we have a direction.

As the caller moves, the connections are handed off to other towers, making the location clearer. Lastly, with the connection to three or more towers officers are able to pinpoint within a degree where that phone was when the call was made.

As Shelly was leaving town, she checked her voicemail, and with that, Detectives were able to obtain her last point. It would seem she was on the highway leading out of town to the South and had stopped at a rest stop not long after being at school.

The Detective's feared the worst as they approached the tall grassy field of the plains of Kansas. Searching the grasslands will not be easy, and we prayed we wouldn't find a body. As Det. White rolled up at the rest stop, he knew the location from the phone could be within 100-200 yards in any direction, but a pit grew in his stomach as he saw Det. Rhino putting on a protective suit, and respirator.

It seemed that something was dead in that area. The smell of rotting flesh filled the air but from where?

The rookie Captain barked, "What are you doing out here? You have cases to clear", to Det. White. Det.

White was not assigned to this case. He jumped in because he wanted to find Shelly for the family (as a friend) and knew he could help. His efforts with Shelly's phone got them this far, but the Captain was riding him about a case he had not cleared.

Apparently, the case of an adult daughter who had stolen her mother's credit card and withdrew a few hundred dollars without permission was more important than a girl's life.

Det. White had identified the daughter and confronted the mother to see if she was going to pursue charges. After she refused to press charges, the bank would not refund the stolen money. After hearing this, the mother complained to internal affairs that she wanted her daughter arrested for stealing her money so she could get her money back from the bank. Det.

White spoke with the prosecutor who confirmed with the mother that she was not willing to sign a complaint for prosecution, and without the cooperation of the mother, they couldn't prosecute the case.

The Captain insisted that Det. White submitted a request for the arrest warrant even though the prosecutor was not going to prosecute the case.

The Captain focused on cleaning up the house cases, issued an ultimatum to Det. White. *"You clear this case with an arrest or get a warrant issued, or I will put you back on patrol."*

White didn't care about pursuing a case that was never going to be prosecuted just to help the mother get her money back from the bank. There were more important things happening, and Shelly's life might depend on his help.

Continuing the search on the grasslands, the stench filled the air as the detectives fanned out searching the source. Lucky they only found a dead deer a few yards off the roadway, but why did the calls and tracking info stop here?

The heat of the day was starting to take its toll on everyone when a rookie patrol officer helping with the search called out that he had found something. The officer was walking on the shoulder of the road headed South out of town when he found a broken cell phone. Det. White was able to match up the service on the phone from Shelly to the EIN (serial number) on the phone found. So, they had her phone but where is Shelly, and why did she ditch her phone?

"Crap", was the consensus within the crowd of detectives. Det. White immediately headed back to the police department to issue more warrants. The new warrants went through fast, and on the following day, information started coming in, but this time they were tracking the perp on his phone.

From the early calls they were able to show that he had been in Mississippi, but had he traveled to Kansas? The address in Mississippi was a trailer on his family's property in a rural part of Mississippi. The calls were all from that location, constantly pinging the same tower, never moving, until the day before Shelly went missing. Det. White was able to show that he had in fact, traveled to Kansas seemingly driving straight through without stopping. Once in Kansas, his phone stopped at the address for Walmart, where they speculated that he got some sleep and supplies for the return trip. On the morning of Shelly's disappearance, he had one call to her phone, then nothing until mid-afternoon when it started pinging in Missouri headed South. Det. White followed the ping until it arrived back in Mississippi, where it had originated. In a coordinated effort with the local Sheriff in the area they were able to locate Shelly, and the perp at the trailer. 72 hours had passed since she disappeared from Manhattan, Kansas, and so much can happen in 72 hours.

Detectives learned that the perp had been grooming Shelly for months to move to Mississippi with him with the promise of a better life, and his proclaimed love for her.

The reality was that he was controlling her every move and action. Immediately after he picked her up from the school parking lot, he started making demands. He directed her to cut all ties with her past which meant throwing the phone out the window.

Once they got to the trailer, he bound her with rope and locked her in the trailer, talking about how he was going to make her his wife and break her in for work. We can only speculate what the "work" might have been, but Shelly knew it was not going to be pleasant. Shelly and the family were extremely grateful for the efforts of the detectives, and they would never know what Det. White sacrificed to make it happen.

✪   ✪   ✪

Closing time at KFC, the young face fry cook was trying to make friends with the part-time college girls working the night shift. The girls only laugh at him, *"You're not a man"* they would tell him. At 6'2", 250 pounds, he was not small, but his demeanor and his face were both resemblant of a 12-year-old boy who had no idea what to do with a girl.

Kevin turned his efforts towards making friends with the night crowd who hung out in the parking lot every night. The "goth" crowd accepted him, and even after a few nights of drinking with them, he became more included in their conversations.

The conversations revolved around the topic of finding marijuana or meth. When Kevin heard this, his ears perked up like a little puppy. He enjoyed meth while in Mexico, and he liked how it made him feel. His newfound friendship placed him on a familiar path. He found himself ditching work to break into cars until the point he no longer had a job or legitimate income to help his mother.

It didn't take long for him to wear out his welcome with his mother, his drug habit, stealing, and outbursts of anger were more than she could handle, so she kicked him out.

Kevin had nowhere to go, so he resolved to live under the trailer with hopes his mother didn't realize where he was, or she would have called the police to have him removed.

Kevin eventually made friends with Jake Adams in the mall where they were playing video games, and Adams told him he was looking for a roommate. Adams knew Kevin was between jobs but gave him a chance to find a job and continue as his roommate.

Kevin was getting his life together again, now that he didn't have any money, and his goth friends didn't talk to him as much. He was going to try to get another job, and with his new friend Jake giving him a place to stay. He was optimistic. The relationship with his mother, Marion, was strained from all the trouble he had been causing with his goth friends, stealing, and getting high. Kevin had made several attempts to talk to her and visit his little sister, but each time it turned into a screaming match, and Marion threatened to call the police. In Marion's eye, she saw too much of Gavin in Kevin. Even Though he was not Gavin's kid he had greatly influenced the man Kevin had become.

Kevin was unable to find work, but he had a friend in Melissa, a waitress from Bob's Diner who was helping him, so he could pay Jake something for the rent even though it was Jake that was buying all the food, and Jake's parents who were paying the power bill.

This arrangement didn't last long before Jake's parents started to pressure him to find a new roommate. It wasn't that they didn't like Kevin, they thought he was sweet and naive, but the fact that he was not working or helping pay the bills left them little choice. On June 9, 2007, Kevin had asked Melissa to come over, and when she pulled up, he met her outside. He explained that he needed to sell a few of his things to have some money for Jake. He quickly went back into the trailer and returned with a nice Kansas State University blanket and a pillow from the couch. She thought this was odd, but then he had returned from the trailer again with about 125 DVDs, and a PlayStation game console. He asked Melissa to take him to the Manhattan Pawn Shop where he pawned most of the items for $110.00.

The two of them drove to Junction City where they partied in a cheap hotel, the Homestead, most of the day. That night they were met by other friends of Melissa until she said she had to return to Manhattan to work. The three guys partied into the early hours swapping stories of their boldest thefts and how close they had each gotten to getting caught. Even for a cheap hotel, they still had some standards, and when the three got too drunk, too loud, and rude to the staff, they were asked to leave.

Somehow, they made their way back to Manhattan, and they dropped Kevin off at his mother's trailer, where he crawled under the trailer with the pillow he had stolen to sleep. By 3 am the night cold had taken its toll on him, and the KSU blanket he had stolen just wasn't enough to keep him warm.

He decided to walk back over to Jake's trailer as if nothing had happened. Little did he know that Jake had called the police to report the theft. Jake had reported that he suspected his roommate was the thief since he had asked him to leave the day before for lack of his ability to pay rent.

Kevin walked up to the door, but then walked away, ashamed of what he had done to the friend who had done nothing but helped him.

The cold air changed his mind, and he knocked on the door. The door opened after the third round of knocking on the door. Jake initially only opened the door a few inches to see who was there, and then Kevin spoke insisted Jake let him in because he was freezing. Jake opened the door all the way, and to Kevin's surprise he was hit square, in the face by Jake.

✪ ✪ ✪

At 8:30 AM, Officer Tony Docka decided he would start his shift by revisiting the theft report he had taken the day before from Jake Adams. Jake had told him that he had a serial number for the stolen PlayStation console, and if he could find the PlayStation, a serial number would positively identify it and maybe the suspect too.

The neighborhood was a generally quiet trailer park area just outside an area of smaller homes. As Officer Docka turned onto the street, he saw the victim's Jeep driving away in the opposite direction with someone much larger than Jake driving. Hoping to talk to him, he thought he might be able to just catch up with him to ask him the questions he needed to finish his report.

The Jeep increased its speed and made several turns through the neighborhood until Officer Docka could no longer tell which way he had gone. It wasn't a police pursuit, but was a very odd and deliberate act to lose the police, thought Office

Docka. He returned to the trailer just in time to see the Jeep had returned, and the driver who had been wearing a red shirt was walking off into the wooded area between two neighborhoods and changing his shirt to blue.

The more Officer Docka thought about it, the more it seemed the person he had seen matched the description of the suspect, Kevin Ruez. Officer Docka called the victim's phone, which went straight to voicemail, so he then went to knock on the door of the trailer. No Answer.

Officer Docka called Jake's father, who had been present during the police report and asked if someone else was driving the Jeep. He replied that no one else was allowed to drive it, that his insurance didn't permit it. Officer Docka looked at the Jeep while he was talking to Mr. Adams noted a cellphone in the Jeep along with plastic tote containers and what looked like a lot of dirty laundry piled in the back. Mr. Adams, concerned for his son's safety, decided to respond to the house to check on his son.

When Mr. Adams arrived, he saw Officer Docka, who had just called into his supervisor to explain what had happened and was advised that since Mr. Adams was the actual renter, he could gain entry into the trailer to do a welfare check on his son.

They tried the door, but it was locked, but Officer Docka found an unsecured window to gain entry. The Sergeant arrived on the scene and assisted the officer through the window to unlock the door. Mr. Adams and the officer walked through the trailer, noting it was a mess, but they could not locate anyone inside. Lastly, Mr. Adams said he didn't think that there had been more items taken, the TV was still in the living room, and other than that there was not much of value to take.

The sergeant departed, leaving the officer to continue speaking to the father. They both looked into the windows of the Jeep, and Mr. Adams permitted him to open the passenger door that was unlocked.

Officer Docka picked up the cellphone and asked if it was his son's, to which Mr. Adams replied "NO." The officer clicked the button to open the rest of the doors as he looked a little closer at the contents in the backseat area. Most of it just looked like white trash bags, dirty linens, and laundry. When he got to the back hatch, he saw a liquid in the bottom of one of the bags, still thinking it was trash. With his ASP baton, he pushed a bag aside and saw what looked like blood on a blanket covering a plastic tote. When he popped off the lid to the tote, his stomach sank to the ground, more worried the father would walk around, he closed the hatch.

Officer Docka thanked Mr. Adams and asked him to go home. He would call him later after he located his son.

Officer Docka was now in a panic. He was not trained for this, and it scared him. He called the Sergeant on the radio, notifying him to return to the scene that he had a 10-40, which is code for a dead body.

The Sergeant returned and asked where he saw the body. The ghost-white officer pointed to the Jeep. He walked the Sergeant to the Jeep, opened up the back hatch, and lifted the lid to reveal a severed arm and a head, which they speculated was Jake Adams.

The two cordoned off the crime scene with yellow tape flapping in the wind and called for the CSI team.

The team responded with a sense of urgency fitting to the situation. They now had a killer on the loose and little information to work with.

CSI noted that when they first walked into the trailer, just as Officer Docka did, there were no obvious signs of foul play, but as they started turning on lights, and started taking a closer look the scene got ugly. Officer Docka was walking them through what he had seen when he was looking for Jake Adams.

He explained that they had used flashlights, and now when they turned on the lights, a drop of blood fell on his uniform. Where did that come from? They both looked up to see the entire ceiling was painted with blood now dripping to the floor and on the seemingly clean bed. There was no bedding on the bed, and there was too much blood for it to be that clean, so they pulled the mattress together to find the opposite side drenched with blood, mostly in one spot as if that was where the body laid.

When they walked down the hall to the other room, they bypassed the bathroom, and he explained that he had not looked in the bathroom during the search for Jake.

The bathroom floor was covered in towels, and the bathtub had a pink hue where an attempt was made to clean up a mess, presumably blood.

Detectives combed the area and every inch of the house, but no real clues of who they were looking for. The only lead they had was that Jake had made the burglary report after telling Kevin Ruiz that he had to move out. Officer Docka's description of the person driving the Jeep was that of a large person, nothing more since he never got close enough to tell if they were male or female.

CSI Det. Gregory received the most gruesome task of processing the Jeep and documenting the contents. The Jeep was towed to the police department, to clear out a maintenance bay in the garage. The bay was then lined with plastic and white sheets with the doors locked, so nothing was disturbed.

Detective White walked briskly to the garage for more information as he had been told a cell phone was found inside the Jeep. Det Gregory in the garage gasped out loud as he started pulling the contents out of the Jeep, starting where Officer Docka found the tote with the head. Each tote contained another part, and with the help of the coroner they were laid out on the sheets and documented. They were building a meat puzzle, and luckily, neither of them had ever met Jake Adams so he was just that, a puzzle. The emotional trauma of working a gruesome case such as this with someone you know could leave scars that would never heal.

Det. White paused as he walked into the bay. It only took a glimpse of what Det. Gregory was doing to start a flood of memories. His mind raced back to Iraq driving through the areas which were heavily bombed by the American sorties. Nothing was more unsettling than the carnage on the highway to hell which used to be the highway exiting Kuwait. The American forces had bombed it as the Iraqi Republican Guard was moving forces in and out of Iraq and Kuwait. With the initial push into Iraq complete the Iraqi Republican Guard had retreated to Baghdad. The 1st Aviation unit after this initial push was diverted to the area just outside the border of Kuwait and forced to land all the aircraft. The winds had changed, and the smoke from the burning oil fields filled the air. The smoke was so thick the light of day shifted to a faint glow, and it seemed more like a night with the moon peeking through the clouds. This condition lingered for days, and the mission of his unit changed if only for a few days.

Then Sergeant White was tasked to clear a path back into Kuwait, working with ground units until the aircraft could resume their mission. Ground units with great intestinal fortitude pulled body after body from the vehicles scattering the highway lining the bodies in the median. Engineer units followed and pushed the vehicles to the left and right to clear the roadway for the allied traffic making their way into Kuwait.

Sergeant White received his task, and it was not a pleasant one. All the members of his platoon were senior NCOs (non-commissioned officers) and

Warrant Officers who on normal days would have been test pilots and aircraft inspectors. On this day, they were corpsman tasked with trying to identify bodies. Not who they were as a person, but merely identifying if they were civilian, military, or unknown by applying a simple colored tag on the body. Green, Red, or Yellow.

Detective White in the garage bay turned away out of view of the evidence being assembled to clear his head of the imagery, making his stomach churn. He called out to Det. Gregory for the cell phone from the Jeep to avoid reentering the bay.

Det. Gregory handed him the cell phone found in the Jeep since the father said it was not his son's, they hoped it belonged to the suspect. They were correct, Det. White was able to get a search warrant quickly to access the phone and found that it belonged to Kevin Ruiz's mother Marion. The text messages and names on the phone were people known to associate with Kevin, but nothing to suggest this was a planned event.

APB (All Points Bulletin) was issued for Kevin with every available unit in the area knowing he was on foot.

The body was slowly pieced together. Feet and legs were separated from the torso, arms, and hands too. The bucket which had contained one of the hands also had the penis in the bucket and the hand was seemingly gripping the penis.

The head which was found first in a tote with the left arm was badly beaten in the area of the eyes and forehead so much so that it was very difficult to make out what Jake might have looked like. Det. Gregory compared Jake's driver's license photo to the face before him. Hair, eye color, and a general shape of his face suggest this was Jake, but the coroner would have to make the official identification. Det. Gregory paused as he placed the head on the top of the puzzle. There was something in his mouth. The coroner pried open his mouth only to find a piece of flesh. He looked at it closely, then moved his hand with the flesh over the area of the mangled genitals and proclaimed that this was Jake's scrotum.

✪ ✪ ✪

The Search Patrol cars flooded the area around the crime scene, and a subject who they now believe was Kevin Ruiz was seen walking away from the Jeep containing the dismembered body of Jake Adams. Kevin walked into a

wooded area behind the trailer originally wearing a red shirt then changing it to blue as he walked out of sight of Officer Docka. The red shirt was found in the area covered in sweat but no blood. Strange, why did he change his shirt?

Dogs were barking in every direction, not helping the K9 unit now on the scene who was trying to pick up a scent. They followed the scent through the small patch of woods into the next neighborhood to a corner then it seemed to disappear. The K9 unit circled the area for hours but could not determine a direction from the corner, almost as if an accomplice had picked him up at this spot.

Det. White received this information, and he decided to look in another direction to recover a possible alternative phone. He reached out to Mr. Adams, who had now been made aware of the possible death of his son pending identification. He asked what phone Kevin could have taken from the Jeep, and they both realized it was the same phone and number Officer Docka had called attempting to reach Jake. With Jake's father's consent, Det. White started a search for the missing phone.

Det. White pinged the phone and it was on the move. It had initially shown a location near the crime scene, but almost 4 hours had passed since then. The phone had called a number which seemed familiar but was not a number the father knew. Det. White realized that it was Melissa's number, but the call was only two seconds, not long enough for a conversation. A second call was made a minute later, and this number was in the system as it belonged to a local taxi company. The next ping on the phone showed a location only two blocks from the police department. Was he turning himself in? The ping was at the intersection, which led to the police department. There is not much at that spot. Panera Bread, a laundromat, a sports bar, then if you go right, there is the police department, and if you go left there is a movie theatre. If you go straight there is a section of woods which leads to the creek, and the backside of another trailer park.

Which way did he go? The phone was offline. Is he coming in to surrender? This last ping was only 20 minutes ago. We need more information. The Detective quickly reached out to his Lieutenant, who was coordinating the search. Within minutes, the area was flooded with patrol cars and detectives walking door to door near the intersection in plain clothes looking for witnesses. The taxi company dispatcher was not much help. All she could provide was that he had been let out of the car in the parking lot near the laundromat but provided the name and the location where the driver could be found since he was currently going to pick up his next fare.

A patrol officer spotted the taxi driver as he was pulling out of the local Dillion's grocery with a sweet little old lady in the back seat. I'm sure he scared the wits out of the old lady when he turned on his lights & siren to make him stop before making it to the street.

"Please don't be alarmed, mam," he said to the passenger, *"we need to talk to your driver for a minute."*

The driver, a Nigerian refugee in the US fleeing a hostile takeover of his village two years ago, was a regular face for the police. He often provided tips about his passengers, fearing they were involved in criminal behavior. He explained that the fare he had picked up in the neighborhood was soaked in sweat, and he said that he and a friend had been playing football. He took the fare to the intersection by the police department, where he was told to stop, and he got out and paid him in cash.

The officer asked, *"where did he tell you to go?"*. The driver explained that the young man had said that he was going to the trailer park behind the movie theatre, but didn't know the address, then told him to pull over at the intersection that led to the police department.

At this point, the driver said he was getting the call to pick up this sweet lady and left him there. Which way did he walk?

"Left," he said towards the trailer park.

"What was he wearing?"

"A blue shirt, and jeans, I think."

"Now, can I take this lady home, sir?" he asked.

The officer collected his contact information for a statement at the end of his shift and let him proceed.

Det. White was unable to find any connections to either Kevin or Jake in the trailer park where he might have gone. Det. White tried the phone search again. It had been 20 minutes since the phone last registered a ping. To his surprise, there was another short call, only a few seconds, again not long enough for a conversation, but this call was to Marion Johnson. Now we had another location on the ping, but this time it was very troubling. He was in the movie theatre, where we had many more potential victims if he decided to fight.

Det. Black walked up to the ticket window with a photo of Kevin and asked if he had purchased a ticket.

"Yes,", to Hostel II," the employee replied.

"When is it over?"

"In about 45 minutes", she said.

Now the detectives develop a plan to hide in the shadows of the theatre and wait for him to go as far away from the public as possible.

The closing credits roll, and to their surprise he leaves with the first group exiting. They cautiously follow and radio ahead to the tactical team outside to be ready. As he exits, he is taken into custody without incident or struggle, almost relieved that he had been caught.

✪ ✪ ✪

CONFESSION

A tear-filled Kevin's left eye where he had just been punched. Jake was not that big, but damn that hurt thought Kevin. At that moment, he knew Jake was on to what he had done. Kevin 6'02" was much larger than Jake at 5'06" and forced his way into the trailer mad from the blow he had just received to his eye.

Jake threw a few more punches in desperation as he was being forced backwards through the living room area of the trailer. Kevin scuffled through the living room, kicked a hammer on the floor and then seeing what it was, he bent down to pick it up. One last blow from Jake landed on Kevin's ear, making it ring but otherwise seemed to do little to stop the pursuit. Jake retreated to his room down the hall with Kevin following after. The attempt to shut and barricade the door was fruitless. Kevin was too big and easily pushed it open.

In the dark room, Kevin swung the hammer and connected with something in hopes it was Jake to make him pay for the blows he had inflicted on his face.

Kevin swung the hammer again. This time he knew, he hit Jake in the head and swung at his head again and again until he heard Jake fall backward into the bed.

Satisfied he had caused enough damage to get his point across, Kevin went to the living room and lit a few cigarettes on the couch. He sat in the darkened room with only the sounds from the wind outside and a new unfamiliar sound. Kevin listened closely and realized it was Jake. Kevin stood up with his head buzzing from the blows inflicted by Jake and a ringing in his ear. Kevin returned to the bedroom, but this time he turned on the light, and realized what he had done with those wild blows in the dark.

He was now looking at Jake face up on the bed, his arms and legs were twitching wildly, and his face was indistinguishable. He had hit Jake in the head and faced several times with the hammer, and Jake was struggling for every breath. Panicked, Kevin went to the kitchen where he got a large knife and returned to the room. Certain Jake was going to die, he softly told Jake sorry, and stabbed at his chest one time.

To his surprise the knife didn't go into his chest very far, so on the second thrust, he put much more force behind it. It seemed like he had stabbed all the way through Jake. But it did the job, Jake quit twitching, and he stopped breathing. Jake was dead.

Kevin again returned to the living room to have a cigarette to think about what he would do next.

Earlier that day he told Melissa that he wanted to see the new Hostel II movie and remembered a scene from the 1st movie. In the movie they cut a body up into pieces to dispose of it and not get caught. Somehow Kevin thought this would be a good plan for what to do with Jake's body.

Kevin collected all the containers he could find. A big blue plastic container, a bucket, and a bunch of trash bags would have to be enough.

He pulled Jake's body on blankets into the bathroom and into the tub, making sure not to make a blood trail along the way.

How should he start? Having worked at KFC, he had cut up a few chickens and thought a person's joints should be similar.

He started at the wrist with the same knife he used to stab him in the heart, but it seemed too big for the job. He got a smaller and sharper knife and was able to work through the wrist joint as he had envisioned from the chicken. He continued with the other wrist, and then went for the shoulders and then the feet. He put the parts into the containers as he worked to make Jake's body small enough to scatter down the Big Blue River before it fed into the Kansas River.

There was a perfect spot where he used to camp when his mother kicked him out before it got cold at the end of Knox Lane. There the water moved fast, and there were several deep holes full of catfish that could make a meal out of the parts.

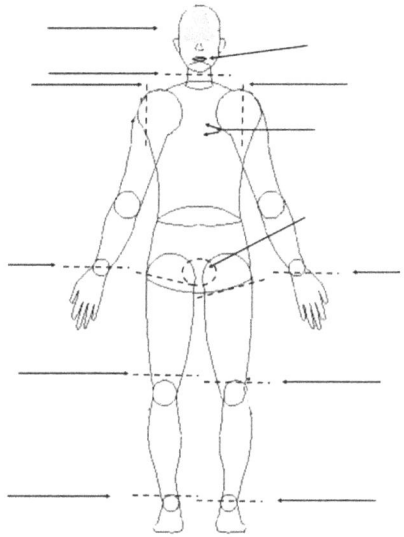

When he got to the groin to cut off the legs, he got homophobic and decided to cut off his penis and scrotum. He took the penis and threw it into the bucket, but the scrotum he decided to put in Jake's mouth. Cutting off the legs at the groin and knees took a lot of effort. He abandoned the idea of cutting the torso in half. Lastly, he took the head. He was disgusted by what he had done to Jake. He was his friend and had given him a place to stay even though he knew Kevin didn't have any money.

Kevin took a moment looking at him, but he had gone this far. If he didn't finish, he would get caught. He started working on the back of the neck but found that the spine was really tough to cut through. He had to get the big knife again and use it like a machete to get the head severed from the torso.

Kevin paused for a moment with sweat running down his nose and looked around him. There was blood all over the bathroom. The only thing that kept it from being a total mess was the now blood-soaked bedding he had used to drag the body into the bathroom. Kevin retraced his steps to the bedroom, looking for blood and wiping it up as he went with the bath towel. In the bedroom the only blood he noticed was on the bed, so he just flipped the mattress, and called it good.

Satisfied after wiping up the bathroom and putting everything in trash bags he was ready to dispose of the body.

He found some clothes in his old room and changed his shirt, now covered in blood, not taking note of his pants which seemed to only have a few spots. Kevin loaded the containers in the Jeep, covering up the containers and the trash bags filled with bloody towels and clothes with another laundry he found in the house.

Just as he pulled out and was heading for the river, he realized that a police car was now behind him. *"Shit, what do I do?"* he thought, but somehow maintained his composure and just drove around the block trying to lose his tail without being obvious.

He realized that if he left the neighborhood, he would be in the open with nowhere to run, so he decided to ditch the Jeep and walk away on foot.

He doubled back to the trailer, parked the Jeep, and grabbed Jake's phone in the console mistaking it for his, as he casually walked away changing his sweat-soaked shirt he went.

Kevin sat down on the curb and pulled out the phone from his pocket. *"Shit, this isn't my phone".* He thought as he struggled to think of someone to call. The only numbers he had committed to memory were Melissa and his mother. He dialed Melissa's number but hung up as soon as it started to ring. *"What would he tell her? Why was he using Jake's phone?"*

He didn't have any answers. He then started scrolling through the numbers Jake had in his contact list and found a number for a taxi, *"this will work"* he said out aloud as he pressed the button to dial.

It was not long before the taxi arrived, but where to go? This was the next problem. His mind raced at this question, but all he could think about was what he had just done to Jake. This gave way to the thought which led him to cut apart the body in the movie Hostel and told the driver to take him to the trailer park by the movie theatre.

Kevin walked to the theatre, but the movie had already started so he decided to sit in the lobby and wait for the next showing.

After the movie, he really had no plan on what to do, and his decision was made for him as he was met by the SWAT team outside. Relieved, he followed their commands and went peacefully to the transport van. A small pocket knife with built-in scissors was the only thing he had on him besides the cellphone and $15.50 cash left from the money he took from Jake.

At the police department, he saw the familiar face of Det. Black entered the room, and again he was relieved since he knew her, and he could tell her what happened.

As casual as any conversation, he walked him through the events which led up to the murder, and everything he did. In the end, he walked him downstairs to the jail to be booked, and he somehow looked so out of place with all the hardened criminals. He had the face of a little boy and a demeanor to match but yet was capable of doing such a violent crime.

CHAPTER 15

DEATH

As a reporter Logan Tyler had been following Kevin Ruez, taking notes when his name came up in the police blotter knowing one day that one thing he was missing would present itself. He knew deep down he had a story with him, he just couldn't fill in the gaps. The story was there, he knew it, he could feel it, but he just couldn't see it yet.

It had been 2 years since Logan's trip to Mexico, and the story had changed a lot. Kevin was now sitting in the jail in Manhattan, Kansas alone and destitute behind bars. Not for the petty crimes he had committed, not for his meteoric rise through the drug ranks from his old days in Mexico, but as a result of following the footsteps of his *infamous* stepfather, Gavin Johnson.

Kevin is a murderer too and not just a murderer, but one whose murderous path had very few details released due to the nature, and means of the murder through which he had committed them- a series of horrifying acts of terror that even the bravest of men in this world would tremble at the sight.

In the days leading up to his trial, Kevin had several conversations with his attorney. Although he had confessed, his lawyer was doing his best to mitigate the circumstances of his client's impending jail sentence. On one such visit, the attorney heard a story of indescribable cruelty that he just couldn't wrap his head around and knew instantly to trust his guts that it would be wise to let the detectives hear about the story too.

Detective Black received the message and coordinated the visit with Kevin in the jail alongside the presence of his attorney. Considering the acts of terror, he had committed, the jail staff insisted that the meeting take place within the confines of the jail facility, and not upstairs in the normal interrogation rooms.

Since the attorney was present, the conversation would be considered a non-privileged discussion. So, the Detective set up a camera to record the conversation. She had no idea what he was going to say, but the attorney was so taken aback by the comments he was insistent on the Detective hearing it firsthand from Kevin.

It's 10:30 am. The moment of truth is fast approaching.

Detective Black makes a call to the jail control room and motions to the camera that it is time to bring Ruiz to the Attorney Room. This was a room where attorneys often sat with their clients to discuss their respective cases. It was not a very big room - just big enough for a small table and a chair on each side. The inmate's chair and table were bolted to the floor, I guess the designer for the room must've seen enough cop movies to know the inmates can't be trusted, and that their attorneys' safety was just as important as any member of the jail facility.

If the inmate was enough of a troublemaker, the inmate would then be put in a separate room with a plexiglass window between them and their attorneys, and a guard would stand at the door to oversee the interaction. Surprisingly, Kevin was very docile in his behavior.

Against all odds, Detective Black managed to fit in a third chair inside the room. The attorney explained that his client's story, Kevin's story, will have no bearing on his charges, but that it might help him reduce or improve his sentencing.

A camera pointed at Kevin as he opened his mouth and began to talk. Kevin started, *"Det. Black, I'm glad it is you coming here to listen to this, I'm not sure anyone else would believe me."*

The Detective did not utter a word. She crossed her arms and stared back at Kevin – eager to learn about what it was that it was so important she needed to come and hoping to find clues that could bring light to several unsolved cases that were assigned to her department.

She listened to the story and was as amazed to find that it was just as chilling as the attorney had described. Detective Black contemplated the information Kevin had just given her about, yet another crime confessed by Gavin Johnson. She asked Kevin if he knew what Gavin was talking about. Kevin replied, *"No, I just thought he was trying to scare me all these years, but after what he did to my mom, I believe it could be true."* She followed up asking if he had ever mentioned it again or gave him any idea when it happened.

Again, he said he barely remembered the story until he was sitting in the jail with nothing but time to think, and the attorney asked him a question about Gavin hurting him when he was a kid. He explained that he didn't know anything about the baby dying, but figured it was something important that he felt he needed to tell the attorney.

The attorney turned to Detective Black and asked. "Does this mean anything? Was there a baby killed?"

Before she would answer, Detective Black took a long pause: *"I'll look into it, I'm not sure"*, said the Detective as she opened the door, and slammed it shut behind her, leaving them to finish their private meeting.

Detective Black's mind was racing "Could it be?" she thought. Was this the case Det. White had with Gavin Johnson so many years ago? He had told her when it came up in the background investigation on Gavin that this case being closed as an accident never really sat right with him. As a rookie at the time, there was nothing he could do, and now maybe he was right to suspect something. "If it is true, we have another murder to charge Gavin Johnson with."

Detective Black walked into the investigation office asking the secretary where Detective White was, "He is downstairs in the evidence room", she replied.

As Det. Black was walking down the stairs, Det. White ran into her on his way up. *"How did it go? What did Kevin have to say?"*

She replied, "You won't believe this, Gavin confessed to Kevin that he killed a baby, the baby from 20 years ago", she said.

"Holy shit, how do we corroborate it?" he responded.

A FEW DAYS LATER...

Det. Black & Det. White both took a shot at speaking to the mother of the baby. They had reached out early in the investigation for more information, and they were quickly shut down. The mother had moved on with her life and wanted nothing to do with dredging up the past and her dead baby. This was the case on their second attempt too even though this time they had a 3rd party confession to tie Gavin directly to the death of her baby. The pain was too great, and the 20 years that had passed were still not enough to get her to speak out and relive the horrors.

Soon, the story of Kevin's gruesome murder had hit AP wire with little blurbs of information showing up in the local paper. There were few details on the murder, and less about the previous murders involving the murderous crime family. Logan Tyler, an up-and-comer in the world of investigative journalism, had moved on from the Manhattan Mercury newspaper to getting small bits with the Channel 2 news.

He had finally been given a break doing small investigative reports mostly talking about things from the police blotter reports and searching for more information. Logan's reports had started to take a familiar style in how he was presenting them in his 2- minute segments. When Logan heard about Kevin Ruez' and his confession, he knew he had a newsworthy story. Digging up his notes, Logan reached out to Detective White to uncover more about the story from the detective's experience.

✪   ✪   ✪

SPECIAL REPORT

This is Logan Tyler Channel 2 reporting from Manhattan, Kansas. We are reporting here live today outside the courthouse with the story of three people who lost their lives by the hand of one crime family, and their heinous criminal acts, and how we may finally be nearing truth after 20 years of speculation and investigations.

✪ ✪ ✪

As the late Paul Harvey was quoted as saying, here is the Rest of the Story...

In the early hours of a cold January morning in 1992, a little baby took her last breath. We will just call her baby X since she was never able to live her life.

When Baby X went to sleep, neither she nor her mother knew they had a killer in the house. Then 6 months old she woke up crying from a soiled diaper, and hunger only to be met by a new face in her short life. Baby X was said to be found choking on a penny that was fished from her throat but succumbed to the incident and died before she reached the hospital. A young rookie patrol officer Brad White took that call, and the case never seemed right, but still, the case was closed as an accident.

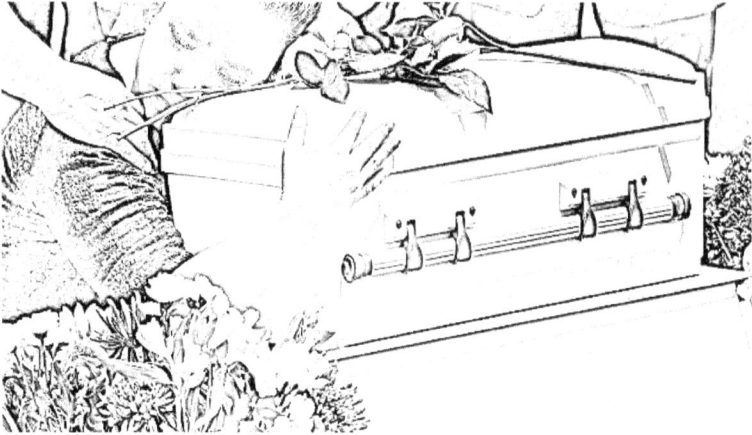

Now fast forward to 2007 and Police Detectives are listening to the story of a baby's death from a whole new perspective. Kevin Ruiz of Manhattan, Kansas - a career criminal who is in jail for his own crimes has confessed that he thought it was important for the Detectives who arrested his Stepfather to know.

When Kevin was still a little boy, Gavin Johnson became Ruiz's stepfather when he married Ruiz's mother. The citizens of Riley County know his name well from his arrest in 2003 for the 1999 murder of 63- year-old Olive Stumpp of Leonardville, Kansas.

Stumpp was found dead in the basement of her Leonardville farmhouse, shot to death. Her death went unsolved for nearly 4 years until Gavin Johnson tried to kill his wife who was the only person who knew he had committed Stumpp's murder. Gavin had confessed the murder details to her in a drunken rant a few years earlier in an effort to scare her and keep her subservient to him. Gavin's confession in the scared mind of his wife was the beginning of his undoing. Gavin's plan to kill his wife was a perfect example of the levels the mind of a true killer will go through to escape justice. In Gavin's elaborate plan he had spent months setting up witnesses, fabricating his wife's desire to kill herself. He purchased chloroform on the internet and had tried to knock her out with it. His wife showed she still had fight in her when she called 911 and dropped the phone for the dispatcher to hear the entire altercation of him trying to knock her out.

Gavin's ego did him in on this occasion as he detailed to Marion that he had planned to knock her out then throw her off the Tuttle Creek Dam making it look like she committed suicide.

The 911 recordings were a key piece of evidence putting Gavin in jail and finally giving Marion the opportunity to tell her story.

Gavin Johnson is currently serving 40 years without probation for the Stumpp murder and another 16 for the attempted murder of his wife, Kevin Ruiz's mother.

Now, loved ones of the deceased baby and detectives on the case are hoping Gavin's ego will help us solve another cold case.

Logan paused for a commercial break on that note feeling he had left the audience on a cliffhanger yearning for "The Rest of the Story."

A few moments later, he continued...

In a special report exclusively here on Channel 2, we have Kevin Ruez on the record, where he will give us his firsthand account of the confession of a killer. *"I think I was about 10 years old when I was living with my mom and Gavin. I remember my mom was out with some friends and I was at home with Gavin. We were just watching TV and everything was fine until he started drinking beer. He started to get angry for no reason. We were watching WWE wrestling, and wrestling around on the floor doing fake moves, until he started getting rough."*

"I told him he was hurting me with a leg hold, and I thought my leg was going to break. He let me go

calling me a wimp but then jumped on top of me pushing my face into the floor until I started to cry. It hurt, I told him, and then he started talking about being able to kill me. He said he knew how he could kill me, and no one would ever know. He grabbed a plastic Walmart bag on the floor and started waving it in my face, saying, "Listen, all I need to do is hold this bag over your face so you can't breathe".

Gavin continued. "After you're dead, I'll sit you at the table with some food on a plate and make it look like you choked on it, and you died." Gavin looked me in the eyes, and with the foul beer breath in my face not 6 inches away he said, *"I did it before. I killed a baby just like this with a bread bag, just because the baby was getting in the way of what I wanted."*

We have found the police report from that January 1992 morning. It was from a grief-stricken mother sobbing while the police talked to a relaxed individual in the name of Gavin Johnson. Johnson's official statement said that he woke up to the infant crying and then choking. He called the paramedics, who showed up within minutes of being called.

Johnson said he had been able to fish out the penny that was supposedly blocking the baby's airway. The infant was taken to the hospital but died while doctors worked to resuscitate her. They found scraping and bruising on the throat that was consistent with Johnson's penny story.

Now with Ruiz's recollection of Gavin's confession comes a new element of a bread bag being used to suffocate and kill the baby, and the possible staging to make it look like an accident.

Kevin Ruiz is currently serving out his own sentence from a 2007 trial case. He was convicted of first-degree murder, aggravated burglary, and residential burglary of the brutal slaying of his roommate, Jake Adams.

In this world filled with cruel individuals who lack compassion for human life, there is a special place for them. We are grateful for the work and diligence of several of our law enforcement officials who stopped at nothing to bring closure to the families and loved ones of the victims.

In an off-camera interview, we had the pleasure and opportunity to speak with Detective Brad White. Det White is the same officer from that 1992 murder of Baby X, and now one of the case

Detectives from the murders of Olive Stumpp, and Jake Adams 20 years later. He explained how humbling it has been to bring this 20-year-old case to a close, but how sad it has been to see the death and destruction caused by Gavin Johnson, and his stepson Kevin Ruez. Ruiz's story will have no bearing on the charges he is currently facing but has brought this 20-year-old murder to light, and hopefully, KARMA will have the final say.

Logan closed saying "Due to special case circumstances Johnson will not be officially charged in the death of Baby X, we hope this report will show that the truth has a way to come out and help bring closure to all the victims of this murderous family.

This is Logan Tyler for Channel 2 News, and that's the rest of the story, Good Night"

STATEMENT OF FACTS

(Statement read at plea hearing by prosecutor)

(This is the actual statement of facts read in open court at the plea hearing. The names have been changed to align with this book, but the facts are real)

On December 15, 1999, at 6:37 a.m. Marvin Stumpp, who resided at xxxx1 Barton Road, Leonardville, Riley County, Kansas, left his home to run a bus route. When he left, his wife, Olive Stumpp, was in bed in the residence as he went into the bedroom and kissed her goodbye. Upon leaving the residence through the North (back) door of the residence, the only door used for access, Marvin Stumpp locked the deadbolt. The front or south door was blocked by a Christmas tree and was not utilized by the family for access. Olive Stumpp was to wait for Marvin's return at approximately 8:15 a.m. who would then take her to work. Olive Stumpp worked at the Leonardville State Bank and was responsible for opening the bank and vault. She was recuperating from knee surgery, and her normal vehicle had been placed in the shop. Due to snowfall the night before, there was a covering of snow on the ground.

✪　✪　✪

Tom Ward travels along Barton Road each morning to go to work. On December 14, 1999, he noted that between 6:30 and 6:45 a.m., he saw a small red car parked along the north side of Barton Road just over the hill to the west of Stumpp's residence, which was occupied.

December 15, 1999, at approximately 6:30 to 6:45

a.m. Ward, made a mental note that again he saw the small red car unoccupied to the west of the Stumpp residence facing east on the south side road on the wrong side of the road, facing so the front of the car was facing the Stumpp residence. The car was gone when Ward returned from work that evening.

Travis Hagerty traveled along Barton Road on December 15, 1999, to attend Kansas State University for a 7:30 a.m. final. Hagerty left his home at 6:30 a.m. that morning. Hagerty stated when he came over the crest of the road. He saw a car backed into the driveway at Gary Wilson's house, which is west of the Stumpp residence. Hagerty noted that the headlights were on, and it appeared to be occupied with one person sitting in the car. The car was a smaller red car. Hagerty said it looked similar to a Honda.

Marvin Stumpp returned home from his bus route at 8:15 a.m., parking the school bus in the driveway to the east of the house. When he got out of the bus, he noticed a set of strange footprints that led around the east side of the house and went to the North door of the house.

Due to curiosity about the strange prints, Marvin went to the house to locate Olive. When he got to the door, Marvin noticed the door was no longer locked. He searched the main and upper level of the house but could not find Olive. Marvin did not immediately check the basement as the door to the basement was shut, and the light to the basement was not on. Marvin did not think Olive would have gone down to the basement after her knee surgery with the pain it would have caused her.

At 8:20 a.m., Marvin called the Leonardville State bank and asked if she had gone on to work. He was told she was not there. He then went to the basement down the stairs to check for Olive. Marvin found Olive lying on her back with blood around her head. Marvin felt her hand, felt that she was very cold, and picked up her glasses he found lying to the north of her head. Marvin then returned upstairs and called 911. The call is recorded as coming in at 8:25 a.m.

Officer Quinton responded, secured the scene, and asked Marvin to check the house for anything disturbed or missing. Marvin looked in a drawer where they kept approximately $100 in twenties in a wallet. The wallet was missing, and the contents of the drawer had been pushed aside. Detectives were sent to the scene and advised by Quinton of the footprints.

The footprints were followed and documented (the map with the footprints was attached). The footprints showed someone had entered the Stumpp property, apparently walked north along a small row of trees, and then paced back and forth behind the Stumpp's propane tank, located just east of the house. The tank is approximately 6 feet in height.

The tracks then proceed to the south door of the house, partially onto the porch, and then back down around the west side of the house to the north door of the house. Upon exiting the north door, the tracks proceed north out of the yard area, into and across a field, across the next mile section of grass and open fields.

Following the path, the officers had to cross through tree lines, over fences, and through the bush. There was a short path of the tracks indicating the person was walking west starting at Barton Road, continuing through the field near the nursing home and stopping at Alembic Road.

By the time the officers followed the tracks, vehicle traffic combined with a slight rise in temperature had caused the tracks to go unnoticed on the roadways. The tracks were distinctive in the pattern allowing the detectives to be sure they were following the same tracks on the course.

Olive Stumpp was found on the concrete floor of the basement with her legs bent one under the other. She was wearing a green Christmas theme long sleeve sweatshirt and black stretch pants. It was later discovered that these things had been put on over her pajamas. It was explained that Mrs. Stumpp would not have responded to the door in her pajamas. There were no signs of forced entry to the home.

At approximately 5:30 p.m. the detectives were notified that the x-rays at Mercy Health Center revealed that Olive Stumpp had been shot in the head. The detectives then began a search of the basement for shell casings. The Stumpp residence at the time was described by the officers as cluttered.

The impending concern for Y2K did not escape this residence. The basement of the residence where Olive Stumpp was located had shelves and boxes everywhere. There were home-canned goods and purchased food stored in the basement. The basement was only a partial 'cellar' type basement with very limited space.

Olive Stumpp had been laying with her feet nearest to the steps coming down into the basement, as if facing the steps when she fell. The detectives located a wooden sink-type table containing many items, located to the right bottom part of the basement. On this table, a shell casing for a 9 mm weapon was located.

A diligent search of the basement then located, among the clutter, a second shell casing within 2 feet of Olive Stumpp's head. The detectives also found a 4'5" mark up the wall farthest from the stairs, consistent with a ricochet mark. (Olive Stumpp's back would have been to this wall based upon how she was found.) The casings, bullet and ricochet mark were photographed as they were found and then collected and preserved as evidence.

An autopsy was conducted by Dr. Erik Mitchell. Dr. Mitchell discovered that Olive Stumpp had also been shot in the upper left chest, 3 inches from midline, in addition to the shot in her head. This bullet traveled front to back, left to right and downward to an exit passing out of the body. This bullet cut the aorta and the 7th vertebra, through the spinal canal and the spinal cord, exiting the vertebral column, and bruising the right lower lung before exiting her body.

Based upon Dr. Mitchell's training and experience, as an expert in forensic pathology, the wound was consistent with where Mrs. Stumpp was standing when the shot was inflicted on her and where the shooter was standing at the time- across the room and slightly elevated from the victim.

The gunshot wound would cause Mrs. Stumpp to fall to the ground. The second gunshot entered Olive Stumpp in her left cheek and traveled into her brain, where it was removed by Dr. Mitchell and turned over to Detective Rhino of RCPD.

The shot to Olive Stumpp's upper left chest would not result immediately in death. Thus, she would still be able to make noise and move. Both shots were close in time based upon the hemorrhaging that was observed.

Detectives unsuccessfully searched for fingerprints and any other type of trace evidence throughout the house. The temperature of the day was noted by Detective Rhino during the investigation at 25 to 30 degrees Fahrenheit. The phone records from the house revealed that at 7:30 a.m., a call was placed from the Stumpp residence to 785-xxx-xxxx.

This phone number went to Security National Bank (now known as Landmark National Bank.) Marvin Stumpp knew of no reason Olive would have been calling that number. At 7:00 in the morning, a call to that number resulted in a recorded message stating the bank's hours of operation.

The RCPF investigation continued by reviewing all open account information for the Leonardville State Bank and the footprints left in the snow.

The shoe patterns from the footprint were used to locate a possible 'suspect' shoe. Detective Rhino unsuccessfully attempted to preserve the print with a casting. Both Rhino and the detectives examined the print, and it appeared to be of a hiker-type boot. Upon observation of the area between the heel and ball of the print, a circle with an "8" was discovered. A waving banner could be seen adjacent to the "8" under closer examination. The banner contained verbiage undetectable from the print in the snow.

It was determined that the pattern was from a shoe sole unique to a Northwest Territory brand boot which was distributed by K-Mart. The pattern included a circle with an 8 on the sole, which was believed to relate to the size of the shoe. The banner bears the words "Northwest Territory" inside it.

A sample pair of the suspect's boots were purchased and used for posters requesting help from the community with information regarding knowledge of anyone wearing similar boots to show prospective witnesses.

The investigation revealed Gavin and Marion Johnson have been experiencing financial difficulties since 1999. Gavin Johnson was spending money, and his bank account at Security National Bank maintained negative balances. He paid minimal payments each month on credit cards. On the date of the murder, the Security National Bank account was a negative -$22.18.

The Johnsons had a child in October 1999, and money was tight. Marion Johnson reported Gavin often took their daughter shopping at K-Mart. He was not working consistently and insisted his wife to stay home with their daughter. Employment records revealed he had six jobs in 1999 prior to December, which he quit or was terminated. Gavin was not working from November 11, 1999, to December 28, 1999. The defendant would periodically deposit checks from Thomas Howard Johnson, later determined to be his father.

On April 5, 1999, Gavin was recorded by RCPD as driving a red Pontiac 4-door vehicle. This car was registered to Arthur Dohr (Marion Johnson's father) and was a 1991 Pontiac 4-door Sunbird. A photograph was located and identified by Marion Johnson as being consistent with the 'little red' car that they owned in 1999. Marion even though the detectives had found a photograph of the car that had been theirs for years.

This same photograph was shown to Tom Ward, who identified the car as the one he saw along the road on December 14 & 15, 1999, facing the Stumpp home.

Marion Johnson told the detectives that back in January 1999, during a discussion about having a gun in the house, Gavin removed a black case which said "Ruger" on it and showed the handgun to Marion Johnson. This gun was used to scare her.

A local pawn record search revealed Gavin Johnson purchased a Ruger 9mm SN#xxx-90033 handgun from Pat's Pawn & Gun on December 20, 1997. The gun was again discussed by Marion and Gavin in November of 1999. Gavin told Marion Johnson that he would take it to his parent's home in Arkansas since she did not want it in their home.

Gavin Johnson opened a savings account with the Leonardville Bank with Olive Stumpp on November 18, 1999. Gavin Johnson was not working at the time and there was no reason he would open an account in Leonardville since it was over 25 miles from Manhattan, Kansas where he lived in 1999.

The Defendant deposited $20.00 to the Leonardville account and submitted signature cards with his and Marion's name on the account. On November 19, 1999, the Defendant pawned the Ruger 9mm SN #xxx- 90033 at Mr. Money Pawn in Manhattan, Kansas. The clerk/owner at Mr. Money, who recorded the transaction, remembered Gavin Johnson, and confirmed that he took the gun from Gavin in exchange for $200.00.

KBI examiner, Dennis McGee, reviewed the Leonardville account documents, the pawn slips from Mr. Money, and the purchase documents for the firearm from Pat's Pawn & Gun. McGee determined it was highly probable that Gavin Johnson prepared the signatures on each of the documents that were authenticated to be his signatures.

At the same time, McGee found that there were strong indications that Marion Johnson did not sign the signature card for the Leonardville Bank account. Marion Johnson denied ever being in Leonardville, signing the documents, or even knowing about the account.

Four days later, on November 23, 1999, the Defendant closed the account at the Leonardville Bank. On December 7, 1999, the Defendant returned to redeem his Ruger 9mm SN #xxx-90033 from Mr. Money Pawn Shop.

The clerk who handled the initial transaction remembered Gavin and prepared the documents for the redemption of the pawn. The ATF required forms for the purchase were completed on December 7, 1999, however the Defendant did not actually recover the gun until December 11, 1999, due to a delay for the FBI required background check to purchase a gun.

The records indicated Gavin Johnson presented a check to the AAFES store located on Fort Riley, showing that he was in the area on December 16, 1999.

It was then time for Gavin to take a trip to Arkansas to visit his parents. Direct TV account records showed there was service for Thomas H. Johnson (Defendant's father) at 620 Johnson Lane, Rison, Arkansas, started on December 18, 1999, following a self-installation of the satellite equipment.

The records indicated Gavin made a deposit on December 21, 1999, into his account at Security National Bank. The check was from Thomas H. Johnson, written to Gavin Johnson and dated December 20, 1999.

Kevin Ruez, the Defendant's stepson, was questioned and recalled taking a trip with Gavin Johnson to Arkansas and installing the satellite dish. Kevin was shown a picture of the 'sample boots' which were identified as being similar in nature to those which left the prints in the snow leading to the Stumpp residence. Kevin knew the boots were the same as those worn by Gavin when he went out and worked.

When Gavin Johnson returned from his trip to Arkansas, he told Marion he had ruined his boots with cement while installing the satellite, so he left the boots in Arkansas. Marion Johnson got the Defendant another pair of boots to replace those that had been *left* in Arkansas. She told the

detectives in interviews in September 2003 that
Gavin Johnson wears a size 8 ½ shoe.

Marion Johnson and the Defendant had been
together since 1991. The Johnson marital
relationship had become strained with verbal
arguments and physical violence consistently in
the home. Gavin Johnson continually verbally
abused Marion Johnson while she was at work
with threatening phone calls of how Gavin would
leave with their daughter before she got home.

Marion Johnson was restricted from all the
family finances by Gavin. She knew Gavin was
not maintaining a job, was using her credit card
without her permission, and he did not allow her
to get their mail. Gavin controlled both Marion
and the household.

In late March of 2003, the Johnsons had a fight at
home. home. After the fight, Marion Johnson left
the house for several hours. When she returned
home, she found Gavin lying face down on the
carpet in the living room. As she got closer to
him, she could smell alcohol.

Marion Johnson reported to the detectives, Gavin
suddenly jumped up and yelled something as if
to try and scare her. She discovered a 12-pack

of discarded beer cans in the trash and said something to him about his drinking.

Gavin told her to *"chill out and that he was fine"*. He then continued the earlier disagreement by telling her that he knew she hated him for everything he had done to her. She would never leave him since they had a daughter together, and they would stay together.

The Defendant told Marion Johnson that if she ever tried to leave him, he would get rid of her. He then told her that he had done it before and would not hesitate to do it again.

Marion reported to Officer Landon on September 11, 2003, that she was frightened by Gavin's threat to her. After Gavin threatened her, he went to the computer pulling up a picture of an elderly woman. He said, *"If you ever leave me, I'll do to you what I did to her."*

The story continued from Marion. She shared with the officer that she did not think Gavin logged onto the internet to access the photograph. She based this upon the time that elapsed and that, if he had needed to log onto the internet, it would have taken more time.

Gavin continued to scare Marion by telling her that a man can kill his wife and get away with it. He then continued to tell Marion about the Stumpp murder. The husband did not kill her, but that he, Gavin Johnson had done it.

Gavin was adamant that he killed Mrs. Stumpp. Marion told her husband that she did not believe him. Gavin continued sharing details of the murder to his wife. The Defendant stated, he had driven around the town (Leonardville) before and knew that the woman's husband drove a school bus. Gavin knew Olive Stumpp worked in the bank. He watched to see when her husband, Marvin Stumpp, left in the morning to drive the bus. Gavin liked Leonardville because it was a small rural town reminding him of home.

Gavin parked his car and walked to Olive Stumpp's house where he knocked on the front door. Mrs. Stumpp motioned for Gavin to go to the back door. When Olive Stumpp opened the door, the Defendant told her his car had broken down and he needed to use the phone. Once she let him into the house, Gavin pulled out his gun and asked Olive Stumpp for the keys to the bank.

Marion listened while Gavin continued with the details. *This is what she relayed to the officer:*

Mrs. Stumpp asked Gavin why he was doing this.

Gavin said, *"Just give me the keys to the bank."* *"Taking my keys will make life harder for you"*, said Olive Stumpp. Gavin got angry with her since she refused to hand the keys over to him.

"If you walk out the door, I will never mention your name and not tell anyone you were here", said Olive Stumpp.

"Those people (Stumpps) lived like slobs. The house was really messy and cluttered and there was stuff everywhere", said Gavin to Marion.

Gavin directed Olive Stumpp to go down to the basement. Gavin described the basement as a grandma kind of basement with canned goods on all the shelves. Olive Stumpp pleaded with him to stop and leave.

Gavin told Marion that when he got to the basement, his whole body went numb. He turned around and shot Olive Stumpp in the chest. He said it did not make a very loud noise and that it was merely a "thunk" sound when he shot her the first time.

Olive Stumpp had a Christmas tree sweatshirt and that is what Gavin shot. He said he started to go up the stairs when he stopped, turned around, and shot her with the gun in the face.

Gavin motioned with his fingers to his left cheek, as he told Marion how he had shot Olive in the face. He described going upstairs, opening the refrigerator, picking up the milk, taking it out, putting it back in the refrigerator, and leaving the house. He told Marion that he walked a very long way, through the snow for a long distance, got in his car, and drove away.

After telling Marion this story of murdering Olive Stumpp, Gavin told her to never mention her (Stumpp's) name again, and to not tell anyone what he had told her. He said it was a joke to scare her.

The story continued with details of Gavin going back to Pat's Pawn and Gun shop to purchase a Ruger 9mm pistol identical to the one he had left in Arkansas (paid $407.73) in February of 2003, over four years after the Stumpp murder. It was noted by the investigators the serial number was xxx-30176.

One month later in March, Gavin pawned this gun at Wildcat Pawn for $200.00. He never came back to redeem his pawn, and the gun was sold.

It was discovered that Gavin Johnson opened another account with Leonardville Bank on April 18, 2003, to then close it on July 29, 2003.

Investigators tracked down purchaser of the Ruger pistol and it was relinquished to RCPD detective Doug Wooden for testing in September, 6 months after Gavin pawned it at Pat's. The handgun was sent to Gary Miller of Sedgwick County Forensic Laboratory, to compare the cartridges, bullets, and firing fired to the crime scene bullets and casings. They did not match.

The investigation then took the detectives to Rison, Arkansas, to file a search warrant in October, to the home of Howard Johnson, Gavin's Dad. Deputy Duke from the Cleveland County Arkansas Sheriff's Office assisted with the execution of the warrant.

When Howard Johnson was advised that the officers had a warrant to search and to retrieve a gun that had been left by Gavin he readily cooperated with a reply, *"is it the 9mm?"*

The detectives confirmed that indeed it was the 9mm, and Howard Johnson walked into bedroom and pulled a plastic bag containing a plastic case from underneath the bed.

Deputy Duke opened the case and found a Ruger 9mm handgun with a serial number ending in xxx- 90033. Handing the weapon to Detective White, it was held onto to be used as evidence in Riley County.

Gavin's Dad, Howard Johnson, was very cooperative and told the officer that Gavin Johnson had brought the gun to his house four years ago, telling him he could have it. Mr. Johnson placed the handgun under the bed in the same plastic bag given to him by Gavin and stored it there for the past 4 years.

The gun was brought to the Arkansas home shortly after Marion Johnson had given birth to their daughter. Gavin only visited Arkansas once in the years and was accompanied by Marion's son Kevin Ruez. Kevin and Gavin stayed a couple of days and left after installing the satellite dish.

Howard Johnson said Gavin had never mentioned the gun again. He did share that Quick Drying Concrete was used for setting the satellite without any spills on Gavin's boots.

✪ ✪ ✪

The Ruger 9mm with Serial Number xxx-90033 was delivered to Gary Miller, Chief of Criminalistics, and a Firearm and Toolmark Examiner at Sedgwick County Regional Forensic Science Center in October of 2003. Gary Miller had over 28 years in law enforcement and had been employed as a Firearm and Tool Mark examiner since 1985- 18 years. His experience included a 16-month firearm and tool examiner apprenticeship, including the study of firearms, ammunition, comparisons, footwear, tires, tool marks, fracture comparisons, serial number restoration, and distance determination. This information demonstrated expertise in every examination performed by Gary Miller.

Miller also trained with the FBI in Quantico, Virginia, on firearms, the Association of Firearm and Tool Mark examiners, the ATF, the KBI and Federal Ammunition Co. Ballistics Training course. He testified for both the Prosecution and defense on multiple occasions as an expert in Firearm and Tool Mark examination. A firearm is cut from metal which is shaved to make the pieces. As the metal is cut, the shavings which are cut away get back under the cutting tool, thereby causing distinctive marks in the firearm itself. Such marks are similar to a fingerprint for a human being. Each weapon will leave a unique distinctive marking on the bullet or casings which are fired from them.

When a weapon is received to compare the bullet and casing to another for comparison and identification, the weapon is test fired into a safe chamber which is filled with water. The water allows for the collection of the test-fired bullet as well as the casings which are ejected from the weapon.

When the officers found the bullet and two casings in the basement of the Stumpp home, it was delivered to the Sedgwick County Lab with the bullet that was removed from Olive Stumpp on December 27, 1999.

Gary Miller examined the bullet and casings originally in 1999 with a report dated January 7, 2000. As mentioned earlier, the casings, bullets, and the Ruger 9mm, Serial Number #xxx-90033 were delivered by Detective Rhino to Gary Miller at the Sedgwick County Regional Forensic Center from the Johnson home in Arkansas on October 27, 2003.

All of the casings, bullets, and the Ruger 9mm were maintained and preserved as evidence during nearly 4 years' time.

Gary Miller re-examined the bullets and casings again. Test fires were conducted from the Ruger 9mm SN #xxx-90033. Upon comparing of the test cartridges to the bullets and casings collected from Mrs. Stumpp and the basement, Gary Miller confirmed, based upon his training and experience, that the Ruger 9mm SN#xxx-90033 fired the two casings which were found in the Stumpp basement. Furthermore, the bullet that was removed from Mrs. Stumpp, as well as the bullet which was found in the basement near her body were both fired from the Ruger 9mm SN#xxx-90033.

✪ ✪ ✪

The review of Gavin Johnson's financial records in 2003 indicated he was still experiencing serious financial problems. The Johnsons were involved in bankruptcy proceedings, had high balances on credit cards, and could only make minimum payments.

As the trial was moving forward Gavin's feet were measured and a cast was made of his feet. His bare foot measured 9 ¼" to 9 5/16". Detective Black also measured the inside measurement of the size 8 Northwest Territory boots which measure 10 3/8".

For example, Detective Black also utilized a Branick shoe measuring device and saw a size 8 boot on the device measured to be 10 inches in length with a standard ruler. Detective Ryan, an officer with RCPD wore a size 8, and he was able without difficulty to put his foot into the Northwest Territory boots, size 8 that were collected as samples.

Throughout the duration of the investigation from 1999-2003 RCPD was careful not to release many of the details of the murder. None of the information about Olive Stumpp's sweatshirt, the location of the shots in her body, the poor condition of the Stumpp residence, or the sequence of the shots fired had been released to the public.

Testimony in the case circled around the evidence that Gavin Johnson went to the Stumpp residence on December 15, 1999 after watching Marvin Stumpp leave on his bus run.

Gavin Johnson had in his possession the Ruger 9mm with Serial Number #xxx-90033, recovered from Mr. Money Pawn Shop on December 11, 1999, 4 days prior to the murder.

Through feigning assistance, Gavin gained entry to the house and demanded Olive Stumpp give him the keys to the bank. When she refused, he ordered her to the basement of the residence.

The autopsy report made it undisputable that after Gavin shot Olive Stumpp in the upper left chest, he intentionally turned and shot her in the left cheek to ensure that she was indeed dead.

The documents from Leonardville Bank verified she knew who he was and proved he intended to kill or murder her when he entered the residence.

HISTORY OF THIN BLUE LINE

The believed origin of the Thin Blue Line is derived from the Thin Red Line, a formation of the 93rd Highland Regiment of the British Army in red uniforms at the Battle of Balaclava in 1854, in which the Scottish Highlanders stood their ground against a Russian cavalry charge. This action was widely publicized by the press and recreated in artwork, becoming one of the most famous battles of the Crimean War.

The "thin blue line" is a term that typically refers to the concept of the police as the "Thin Blue Line" which keeps society from descending into violent chaos. The "blue" in "thin blue line" refers to the blue color of the uniforms of many police departments. The idea is that the police as a necessary presence provide protection from those who when left unchecked would stray from socially acceptable behavior.

The concept that we are all mostly honest law-abiding citizens who only stray when left with no boundaries. Such is the case with locked doors, and signs telling us who should STOP, or YIELD.

The presence of Police adds to those common sets of rules as a form of guidance and eventually gave way to laws with penalties for those who fail to follow the rules.

The job of maintaining those rules puts the Police in the position of being admired when needed and hated when they stand in the way of wrongdoers' personal desires. The obligation of these duties is strained when society deems the job of the police as something different, directing them to let certain offenders go and punishing others unfairly for the same offense.

We all know prejudice is a live force, it is in those of ALL colors mostly from learned behavior in their upbringing or influential subjects in their life. We cannot allow narrow-minded individuals to drive the will of society, we are all equal, and we create our own fate.

The "Thin Blue Line" flag is an all-black flag, bearing a single horizontal blue stripe across its center. Variations of the flag, often using various national flags rendered in black and white with a blue line through the center. This flag had little publicity outside the law enforcement community, where it identified those supportive of Law Enforcement until 2014.

The law enforcement world changed when critics argued that the "thin blue line" represents an "us versus them" mindset that heightens tensions between officers and citizens and negatively influences police-community interactions by setting police apart from society at large. Groups began to view it as a symbol of opposition to the racial justice movement "Black Live Matter".

The reality is that we are all part of the thin blue line, we are those who selflessly engage to stop those attempting to harm others. The arbiters of chaos come in many forms, yes even misguided police officers with poor training or prejudicial upbringing.

We must stop using color as an excuse and relearn what we lost from our innocent youth. We are all the same, and our goal is to live in peace.

ACKNOWLEDGMENT

Special acknowledgments go out to Jennifer Speidel for helping me bring my stories to paper. The Men and Women of the Aviation Training Brigade at Fort Rucker, AL, 4/2 ACR (Armored Cavalry Regiment) Germany, F co. 1st Aviation, BIG RED ONE, Kansas, who taught me how to grow to be a self-confident, meticulous soldier, who stands proudly for our country.

Kansas Law Enforcement Officers of the Junction City Police Department, Sgt. Tim Brown, Jeff Childs, Arnold Foxx (RIP), Alex Johnson (RIP). Kansas Law Enforcement Officers of the Riley County Police Department. Cpt. Gary Grubbs, Detective Allen Rhinker, Ryan Runyan, and Carla Swartz for always being a friend as we bore the unmentionable horrors the world produced.

Together with you I learned what kind of Officer I wanted to be and took that into my private sector career to solve cold cases.

Together I would like to think that we made the world a better place.

ABOUT THE AUTHOR

Brad Schlerf is an American Army veteran, retired police detective, and author. The son of volunteer EMTs and firefighters, Brad began his public service at an early age by becoming a volunteer firefighter himself at age 14 and an EMT at 15. When he was 14, a friend's father taught him to fly a glider plane, starting his interest in flying. He went on to join the US Army Aviation and served for eight years, going on assignments in places such as the border of East Germany and Czechoslovakia, state-side with the Big Red One and 1st Aviation Division, and Iraq and Kuwait in Operation Desert Storm.

After returning from Desert Storm and serving as a quality control aircraft mechanic with Lockheed Martin, Brad took a position with the local police department in Junction City, Kansas. He worked cases involving everything from stolen bicycles to homicide, developed the Gang Intelligence Unit, and even acted as a liaison to the FBI to assist in the investigation of the Oklahoma City bombing of 1995. From there, he moved to the Manhattan Police Department in Riley County, Kansas, and after a few short years was promoted to detective. With the RCPD, Brad developed the Hi-Tech Crimes Investigation Unit shortly after the birth of the internet and, working with a team of nerds, lawyers, judges, white hat hackers, and officers, was involved in the initial stages of what is now Computer Forensics. His assignments spanned over all major crimes, and he served as a liaison to the DEA working narcotics, and on the JTTF (Joint Terrorism Task Force) after the events of September 11th, 2001.

After retirement, Brad has gone on to continue in the roles for public service. He developed his own company, Forensic Solutions Inc. which has divisions that work in Computer Forensics, Voice Stress Analysis for Cold Case investigations, and data recovery for the everyday person. His investigations with FSI have been featured on *48 Hours*, *True Crime TV*, A&E's *Dead Again*, NBC, Discovery Channel's *Killing Fields*, and several journals.

Brad is the author of the *Gotcha* book series, a True Crime trilogy based on real homicides and Cold Cases that he helped solve during his career as a detective.

Brad is married and the father of three beautiful children. Brad continues to hope this world will see past the issues of color and hate and realize we are all in this together as ONE race: Human.

Follow Brad:

BradSchlerf.com
Facebook/gotcha.author
Facebook/BradSchlerfAuthor
Facebook/gotchabooks
Instagram/gotchabooks
Twitter/gotchabooks
LinkedIn/gotchabooks
Pinterest/gotchabooks
TikTok/gotchabooks

COMING SOON

BOOK 2

Gotcha – A Perfect Murder
- Coming Soon ...

BOOK 3

Gotcha – Seeking the Truth
- Coming Soon ...

Visit BradSchlerf.com

www.ingramcontent.com/pod-product-compliance
Lightning Source LLC
Chambersburg PA
CBHW062130040426

42335CB00039B/1869